WOMEN
MEAN
BUSINESS

There's an extraordinary place in the world for women who lift other women. This book is dedicated to these trailblazing women who are transformational leaders, who capture our imagination, and who lift us higher. And to you, so many countless women who drive with positivity, persistence, authenticity, and purpose, we salute you.

And to our readers who pledge to drive change and lift others. We urge all to action, to renewed sisterhood; together, let's accelerate the success of businesswomen. For the three of us, this book is part of our legacy, and we hope it becomes part of yours.

WOMEN MEAN BUSINESS

Over 500 Insights from Extraordinary Leaders to Spark Your Success

Edie Fraser, Robyn Freedman Spizman,
Andi Simon, PhD

Andrews McMeel
PUBLISHING®

CONTENTS

- Lisa Edwards, Executive Chair, Diligent Institute
- Lakshmi Eleswarpu, Global CIO
- Michelle Gadsden-Williams, Managing Director and Global Head of Diversity, Equity, and Inclusion (DEI), BlackRock
- Cindy Kent, COO, Everly Health
- Jill Marcotte, Partner, Chief Supply Chain Officer, Dealer Tire
- Jennifer McCollum, CEO, Linkage, Inc. (A SHRM Company)
- Mia Mends, CEO, C&W Services, a Division of Cushman & Wakefield
- Sherlaender "Lani" Phillips, Vice President, Microsoft, U.S. Channel Sales
- Carla Grant Pickens, Vice President, IBM Global Operations, Platforms, and Delivery

Chapter 4: Business Association Innovators Advocating for Women at Work ... 71

- Karen Greenbaum, CEO, Association of Executive Search and Leadership Consultants (AESC)
- Nicki Keohohou, CEO, The Direct Selling World Alliance (DSWA) and Coach Excellence School
- Susan Neely, CEO, American Council of Life Insurers (ACLI)
- Liz Sara, President, SCORE Foundation
- Deborah Wince-Smith, President and CEO, Council on Competitiveness

Chapter 5: Women Entrepreneurs Creating Bold, Brave Solutions ... 83

- Sue Burnett, Founder and President, Burnett Specialists
- Shital Daftari, Founder and CEO, SNT Biotech
- Molly Fletcher, CEO, Speaker, and Former Sports Agent
- Theresa Harrison, Founder and President, GEORGE STREET Services, Inc.
- Felicity Hassan, Founder, TheFind
- Asma Ishaq, CEO, Modere
- Margery Kraus, Founder and Executive Chairman, APCO Worldwide
- Sharon W. Reynolds, Entrepreneur and CEO, DevMar Products, LLC, and DevMar Manufacturing; a Multi-Award-Winning Serial Entrepreneur
- Ilene G. Rosenthal, CEO and Founder, Footsteps2Brilliance
- Joyce Salzberg, CEO, Sunny Days
- Gemma Toner, Founder and CEO, Tone Networks

Chapter 6: Women Business Creators and Innovators Transforming Ideas into Action ... 107

- Tacy M. Byham, PhD, CEO, DDI
- Tena Clark, CEO and Founder, DMI Music & Media Solutions
- DeLisa Guerrier, Managing Partner, Guerrier Development; CEO and Founder, Storyville Gardens
- Lili Hall, CEO and President, KNOCK, Inc.
- Kate Isler, CEO, TheWMarketplace
- Kimber Maderazzo, Beauty Leader and Activist
- Deirdre Quinn, Cofounder and CEO, Lafayette 148 New York

- Judi Sheppard Missett, Founder and Executive Chair, Jazzercise, Inc.
- Clara Sunwoo, Designer and Founder, Clara Sunwoo; and Roseann Sunwoo, CEO and Founder, Clara Sunwoo
- Kay Unger, CEO, Kay Unger Design; President and CEO, Kay Unger Family Foundation; Chair Emerita, The Parsons School of Design; Executive Board, Retailers United

- Lynne Born, Chief Practice Officer, Aspiriant
- Heather Ettinger, Chairwoman, Fairport Wealth; Founder, Luma Wealth
- Judith Goldkrand, Senior Vice President, The National Women's Segment Leader, National LGBTQ+ Segment Leader, Wells Fargo
- Jill Johnson, Cofounder and CEO, Institute for Entrepreneurial Leadership
- Alexandra Jung, Cofounder and Managing Partner, Amateras Capital; Head of Private Debt, AEA Investors
- Shelly Kapoor Collins, Investment Partner, Sway Ventures
- Kay Koplovitz, Cofounder and Chairman, Springboard Enterprises; Founder, USA Network
- Alexandra Lebenthal, Senior Advisor, Houlihan Lokey
- Loretta McCarthy, Co-CEO and Managing Partner, Golden Seeds
- Kim Moore, Partner, Venture Capital Team, Glynn Capital
- Rachel Vinson, President, Debt & Structured Finance in the United States, CBRE

- Esther Aguilera, President and CEO, Latino Corporate Directors Association (LCDA)
- Subha V. Barry, President, Seramount
- Lorraine Hariton, President and CEO, Catalyst
- Anna Mok, President and Executive Board Chair, Ascend and Ascend Foundation; Cofounder, Ascend Pinnacle
- Irene Natividad, President, GlobeWomen Research & Education Institute
- Pamela Prince-Eason, President and CEO, Women's Business Enterprise National Council (WBENC)
- Sandra Quince, CEO, Paradigm for Parity
- Dr. Rosina L. Racioppi, President and CEO, WOMEN Unlimited, Inc.
- Dr. Sheila Robinson, Founder, Publisher, and CEO, Diversity Woman Media, *Diversity Woman Magazine*
- Monica Smiley, Editor and Publisher, *Enterprising Women Magazine*; President and Founder, Enterprising Women Foundation
- Stephanie Sonnabend, Cofounder and Chair, 50/50 Women on Boards
- Gwen K. Young, CEO, Women Business Collaborative
- Johanna (José) Zeilstra, CEO, Gender Fair

The mission of this book is to help you change your life.

BUSINESS NEEDS WOMEN,
AND WOMEN MEAN BUSINESS

Meet these trailblazing women who want something remarkable for you and all women. These are outstanding individuals inspiring us to reach higher levels of personal achievement. As you read, ask yourself, where am I going? Who can help me get there? How can I achieve and embrace the best possible me? See how far you can dream. And most importantly, use this book to help define what you envision for yourself. What is your wisdom? How will you imprint your legacy? And ultimately, how will you make your life count? Whether you want to be a CEO, lead the C-suite, become an entrepreneur, activist, or philanthropist, or blaze a different trail, success should be obtainable for all women at every stage in their careers.

Every woman in this book has a story to tell, and by no means is this list complete. We aim to share keen business acumen mixed with unparalleled grace and style. The heartfelt generosity of these dynamic women is evident. They want to inspire and guide you while accelerating your opportunities for success—however you define it.

As you read the book, you may want to scan the pages to find familiar inspiring names or select a category of interest. You may prefer to read them all straight through or dip in and out to find inspiration when you need it. Keep coming back to the ones that speak to you. Expand your journal of key phrases or essential insights. Each day, let *Women Mean Business* live with you.

This book is a deep dive into true success and personal achievement. It's up to you how you can apply this actionable wisdom at work, at home, and in life. These women personify the best of what we all can be. We hope to inspire you to follow your own story—the one you write.

You are not alone, no matter where you find yourself on your journey. Let this rare assembly of women help you obtain the grandest prize: a legacy of your determination and passion, knowing that you also supported other women along the way.

We came together to celebrate the power of progress as women are galvanizing the momentum, moving women in business forward faster. Blaze your trail. The time is now, and we have work to do. As we transform our lives, in business and society, let our success shine all over the world.

Edie Fraser
Robyn Freedman Spizman
Andi Simon, PhD

"Remember that leadership is action and not position. Don't measure your success by title. Measure it by impact."

—Carol B. Tomé

CHAPTER 1

CEOS PAVING THE WAY

When the Chief Executive Officer (CEO) or the highest-ranking individual in a company is a woman, she becomes an extraordinary example of what is changing in business. These women are redefining the leadership landscape in enterprises of all sizes and types of industries. Their successes reflect how doors are opening, enabling other women to rise. While we celebrate these women trailblazers, let's understand that there is still a long way to go.

Think about what their pearls of wisdom mean to you. Together their ideas do not become the "magic sauce" to success. Rather, each reflects how women who have become CEOs of major organizations see the world. They believe in collaboration, and they lead with purpose, passion, and with profits. They know it is not one or the other, but these attributes marked their own journeys to the top.

You'll find important reoccurring themes among the wisdom of these accomplished CEOs: Look forward to what is possible. Look around you at the talent who will grow with you. Look inside to find yourself. And believe in what you can achieve.

All these women might have started with a plan but quickly realized that there was no straight line to the top. They were often surprised by opportunities they had not anticipated. And each of these CEOs show how you, too, can pivot as you pursue your promise.

These women have leveraged learning and development opportunities. They are champions for inclusivity, diversity, and equality for all women.

Perhaps most important, these women want you to enjoy your journey, as they have. See the opportunities and believe in your capabilities. Take the chance and envision what you can accomplish.

GLORIA BOHAN

PRESIDENT AND CEO, OMEGA WORLD TRAVEL

Gloria Bohan launched Omega World Travel in 1972. Under Gloria's leader- ship, Omega is considered a pioneer. It has built a strong reputation for quality service and innovative technology in the corporate, government, meetings, and leisure travel markets. Omega ranks as one of the top travel management companies worldwide and one of the largest woman-owned businesses in the U.S., with annual sales of more than $1 billion. With its growth fueled by strategic partnerships, e-commerce execution, and global expansion, Omega's world headquarters are in the Washington, DC, area. Its international headquarters are in central London, with other locations throughout the U.S., Europe, and the Middle East. Gloria founded and owns Cruise.com, one of the largest sellers of cruises on the internet, and TravTech, an industry software development company. She credits her success to her staff and believes in fostering the entrepreneurial spirit.

> "I strive to maintain a positive attitude. A positive attitude enables me to draw on my talents, reach out to others, find their positive energy, help them, and understand their worth."

My Five Wisdoms

1. Look for the talent of other people.

Try to find out what makes them tick. It's important to do this to build a strong team. Business leaders need to help others to find success. Early at my company, we established a "buddy system" as we hired newcomers. They grew with us, were loyal, and became great team members. My human resources department is essential to recruitment.

2. Create an entrepreneurial atmosphere.

It is essential to look for suggestions, and the company needs to let the staff know they will support their efforts when trying new initiatives. We back them up. The residual benefit is discovering new abilities, growth, and a "can do" mindset. When achieving success, the desire to keep achieving becomes the norm, and creativity and innovation follow.

3. Diversify.

A diversified staff will open the door to understanding how to service clients from many different industries and areas worldwide. A diversified portfolio of other parts of the traveling public, including business travel, government travel, meetings, leisure and vacation sectors, and cruises, has enabled us to balance our services and stay strong. Know your customer.

4. Community outreach is essential.

Helping others in the community will bring great rewards. A business needs to support groups that help a community flourish. Get to know the business leaders, educators, and community you will serve.

5. Service excellence is the mission.

Achieve the mission. The Omega mission statement speaks to continuous learning, fostering teamwork, creating an innovative atmosphere, and achieving the unexpected. Make sure your core is strong. To grow, we need to strengthen our core and understand the basics that make us who we are. Our suppliers and vendors must share our mission.

MARIA COLACURCIO

CEO, SYNDIO

Maria Colacurcio is the CEO of Syndio, a workplace equity analytics solution helping modern companies embed workplace equity into their core business to achieve enduring success. As a CEO and a mom of seven, Maria is walking the walk on eradicating workplace inequities. Having started her career in Washington, DC, she has a long history of mission-driven work and spurring change. Maria serves on the board of the nonprofit Fair Pay Workplace. She was named as one of the 100 most intriguing entrepreneurs by Goldman Sachs Builders + Innovators Summit and an EY Entrepreneur of the Year.

> "If you want to make a society work, then you don't keep underscoring the places where you're different—you underscore your shared humanity."
> —Sebastian Junger, *Tribe: On Homecoming and Belonging*

My Five Wisdoms

1. Break away from gender boxes.

Help people switch roles to avoid falling into outdated norms, whether by hiring for skills and potential or by making sure my boys' chores include doing the dishes. This approach fosters a true growth mindset. Engage men as accomplices in the fight for equity. Many of them are in the ring with us. Acknowledge that and activate it.

2. Be relentless about prioritizing your time.

I don't have more time than anyone else. I have an incredibly supportive partner, discipline, and focus. I start my day at 4:45 a.m. with an hour of work, then a workout in the garage before getting the kids out the door. I block off 2:30 to 3:30 on my calendar, so I can be present with them at the kitchen counter when they are the most talkative. Figure out when you're in your flow and when your people are in their flow, and format your day around that.

3. Merge your passions and values with your workplace.

When everyone brings their whole selves to work, the company is better. I've brought my competitive spirit and passion for fitness to the office by holding pre-board meeting workouts with our Board of Directors and employees. It brings us together, making us stronger. Hook into your passions and encourage others to do the same to inspire a sense of community.

4. Lead with relationships.

Leadership is helping others achieve more than they might otherwise. People will achieve more when they know their leader genuinely knows them and cares. Relationships are also what you carry with you when you leave any company or community. As we broaden the definition of good leadership, I hope our relationships will break down outdated barriers to building successful, groundbreaking companies.

5. Embrace the role of CEO—full stop.

People regularly say that Syndio has a female CEO. But as my (male) colleague likes to counter, there's another term for that: "CEO." When do we get to be CEOs instead of "female CEOs"? It starts by calling someone out and shining a light on the inequity of the comment. We'll drive progress with intentional focus and commitment, cultivating fairness at every turn.

JILLIAN EVANKO

PRESIDENT AND CEO, CHART INDUSTRIES, INC.

Jillian Evanko is President and Chief Executive Officer of Chart Industries, Inc. (NYSE: GTLS), serving in this capacity since June 2018 after joining Chart in February 2017 as Chief Financial Officer (CFO). Before joining Chart, Jill was the CFO of Truck-Lite and previously held operational and financial positions at Dover Corporation (NYSE: DOV), Arthur Andersen, LLP, and Honeywell Corporation. Jill serves on Chart's Board of Directors and the board of Parker Hannifin Corporation (NYSE: PH). Jill received a master of business administration from The University of Notre Dame and a bachelor of science from La Salle University.

> "Taking opportunities (even if not promotions) weaves experiences together that give you a broader sense of leadership than staying on one 'predetermined' path."

My Five Wisdoms

1. Don't strive to be the best "female" executive. Strive to be the best executive.

Many times, I am introduced as a female CEO, yet I look to be the best person for the job. This is also how I fill other jobs—diversity with capability and competencies that best match the role we are trying to fill.

2. Create the space for ongoing dialogue with a variety of people.

Answer everyone who reaches out to you. You never know how you will impact them, or they will affect you. I always ask people to connect with me when I present at industry events. This results in unexpected positive outcomes. One was a lady who reached out to me after I spoke about diversity in the energy industry in India. We hired her to run our marketing in India!

3. Take opportunities presented to you, as doors open for a reason.

These may not always appear in a straight line as you look at your desired career path. The jobs may be parallel responsibilities or take you to new geography. Yet they go into making you an experienced executive. Take on a variety of challenges. You become a more compassionate leader. Once, I moved to Indiana (USA) to move a plant from Indiana to Mexico. We had to keep the changes confidential until we could announce them. Knowing this would affect plant team members taught me that we could accomplish change with compassion and empathy and improve the profits.

4. My father always told me not to look for a promotion but rather, "Keep your head down and do your job."

This philosophy has proven to be great advice. I tell others not to expect your team to work harder than you do.

5. You can be a great mom AND a great executive.

I am the mother of a now nine-year-old daughter. When she asks me to deliver a keynote speech, I am proud that my strong leadership influence is reflected in her. Yet I am even prouder when she tells people that she wants to be a mommy (and an author) when she grows up!

SHOSHANA GROVE

CEO AND MEMBER OF THE BOARD OF DIRECTORS, INTERNATIONAL BRIDGE, INC.; CHIEF SALES AND MARKETING OFFICER, SAFEPACKAGE.COM

Shoshana Grove is an award-winning executive with leadership experience in the public and private sectors. As Chief Executive Officer at International Bridge, Inc., she has primary responsibility for driving the company's innovative technology and global parcel delivery strategies. Shoshana serves concurrently as the Chief Sales and Marketing Officer for PreClear.com, a customs compliance and digital auditing platform that serves many of the world's largest e-commerce entities.

Previously, Shoshana served as Secretary and Chief Administrative Officer of the Postal Regulatory Commission; the regulatory body charged with oversight of the United States Postal Service (USPS). Shoshana served for over 30 years in USPS field operations and headquarters.

Shoshana serves on the boards of International Bridge, Executive Women in Government (past President), Package Shippers Association, and Women in Logistics and Delivery Services (Chair) and is a member of the State Department International Postal Policy Advisory Committee and the Advisory Council of Women Business Collaborative.

> "I've learned that people will forget what you said, people will forget what you did, but people will never forget how you made them feel."
> —Maya Angelou

My Five Wisdoms

1. Passion.
Pursue your passion. Sometimes this means finding inspiration and motivation in imperfect situations, relationships, or jobs. Having a positive mindset is the foremost attribute of successful leaders. We all have days when we feel disconnected and discouraged. Success is built on hard work, motivation, and dedication. Authentic passion, commitment, and proactivity come first.

2. Authenticity.
Strive to be present in the moment, and give your full attention to problems, situations, and relationships. Successful business and personal relationships are built on empathy, honesty, and trust. Authenticity is a cornerstone of executive presence. Work on your personal brand.

3. Relationships.
Identify your go-to people. Always help bring others up. Identify successful people who will amplify you as well. Reach out courageously and with confidence. People you admire will be pleased and honored and approve of your good taste. You will reflect on how they became successful!

4. Push the body and clear the mind.
Rigorous activity every day is a cornerstone of success. Exercise clears the mind, instills confidence, stimulates creative thought, and burns off nervous energy, leaving behind positive energy and providing the ability to focus on complex tasks.

5. Volunteerism.
Always, always volunteer—for work assignments that stretch you, for the jobs that no one else wants, for nonprofit opportunities that enhance your experience and résumé, and to help others who need a hand. You will be rewarded greatly. You will make life-long friends who share your values, realize opportunities to be a center-stage leader, and stretch your skill sets. You will make a positive impact on others, and that is its own reward.

BARBARA HUMPTON

PRESIDENT AND CEO, SIEMENS USA

Barbara Humpton is the President and CEO of Siemens USA. She guides strategy and engagement in the company's largest market and leads a team of approximately 40,000 to serve customers in all 50 states and Puerto Rico. Drawing from decades of experience working on global security projects, Barbara views the true purpose of technology as expanding what's humanly possible. She's shared her signature optimistic perspective with audiences worldwide, hosting a podcast called *The Optimistic Outlook* that explores how we'll build a more resilient, sustainable, and equitable future. She's also passionate about diversity, STEM education, and what she calls a work-life blend that honors her priorities at Siemens and as a grandmother.

> "Speak up and be brave. Don't hesitate. Don't hold back your ideas. Ask questions. Believe what you say has value and will make a difference."

My Five Wisdoms

1. Find your purpose.

It's important to ask, "What is your personal 'why'?" I learned early in my career that the true purpose of working with technology is to change the world in a positive way. That purpose has been at the center of my career journey, bringing me to Siemens, where we're focusing our technology and expertise on solving the world's biggest challenges. Let purpose guide how you use your knowledge and skills and find the people and organizations that align with your personal "why."

2. Be your authentic self, and know that is enough.

I was told I wasn't "executive material" in the middle of my career. I was too nice. But I knew I had something to offer, even though I didn't fit the mold. I knew positive leadership had value. I didn't change; instead, what's changed is the idea of who can be a leader and what it means to lead.

3. Replace work-life "balance" with work-life "blend."

Balance implies perfection and equilibrium. Reality is a lot messier, and our priorities often compete. Instead, focus on what matters—addressing business as it arises and looking out for one another. And remember to be kind to yourself so that you can do the things you want to do with and for others.

4. Empower those around you.

One of leadership's most important acts is to let others lead. Recognize that people want to step up and be given more responsibility. By creating a culture of empowerment and belonging, we can foster the joyfulness that comes when you feel trusted and see that your work is valued. Lean into your networks so that everyone can contribute to the larger mission.

5. Raise your hand.

Don't wait to be called on. Stop and think about what you love to do and raise your hand for that kind of job. It takes confidence and optimism to raise your hand, knowing you have the skills and talent to help the situation. Be willing to give it a shot. Because when you raise your hand to work on tough projects, people take notice and will think of you when other opportunities become available.

SHEILA JOHNSON

FOUNDER AND CEO,
SALAMANDER HOTELS & RESORTS

Sheila Johnson is a true renaissance woman, entrepreneur, activist, sports owner, women's advocate, movie producer, artist, philanthropist, wife, mother, and grandmother. As Founder and CEO of Salamander Hotels & Resorts, Sheila operates a collection of luxury properties in the U.S. and the Caribbean that includes the Forbes Five-Star Salamander Resort & Spa in Middleburg, Virginia. A classically trained violinist and self-taught business-woman, she cofounded BET Networks, which became the world's most powerful African American brand.

Sheila's foray into sports—as a Partner in Monumental Sports & Entertainment—made her the first and only African American woman with ownership of three teams, all in Washington, DC: The NHL's Capitals, the NBA's Wizards, and her beloved Mystics of the WNBA.

> "Empowerment is an attitude. Words cannot express how often I wanted to give up and play the martyr rather than pick myself up to fight another day."

My Five Wisdoms

1. Build a network.

Everyone knows about the business leaders' "old boys' network" and "brotherhood." The overt maleness of those terms aside, a woman should never underestimate the power of a rich base of contacts—one she regularly feeds and nurtures. Believe me, it works. Take it from a girl who grew up in Chicago, a city of connections and a place where, famously, if someone's looking for somebody to do a job, the single most uttered phrase is, "I got a guy . . ."

2. There are no small tasks.

Do every job, no matter how small, as if someone's watching. And take special pride in attention to detail. How you do the small things in business will ultimately shape the big ones.

3. Never burn bridges.

I always tell interns and those starting: "Any job you ever accept, even the crummy ones, make it your goal to—at the moment you announce you're leaving—have your boss either (a) ask you to stay or (b) tell you you're always welcome back." So many people see themselves as above a menial job or will let their performance suffer as soon as they choose to leave it. Believe me, that's the career equivalent of lighting a match to the very bridge that helped move you to the next phase of your career.

4. Never stop asking questions.

There's an educational concept called "lifetime learning," built around the belief that the world continues to grow and that the only way to ensure our relevance is to grow along with it. There may be no more powerful business gift than intellectual curiosity. Regularly ask questions. It is the surest way to be written into any equation.

5. Support other women.

Men are always helping each other to climb higher up the ladder. For years, women have done the opposite. It's as though another woman's gain must come at their expense. As real as the words you're reading now, the only person who can put an end to it is the woman staring back at you in the mirror.

SUNEERA MADHANI

FOUNDER AND CEO, STAX

Suneera Madhani is the Founder and CEO of Stax, one of America's top 10 fastest growing fintech companies, catapulting from start-up to unicorn with a valuation of over $1 billion and more than $100 million in recurring software revenue. Suneera has become a notable minority female entrepreneur, breaking countless statistics and raising over $500 million in venture capital. Suneera was recognized as an honoree of *Fortune*'s 40 Under 40 list. She is a recipient of EY's Entrepreneur of the Year award and featured in *Bloomberg, Fortune,* and more. Suneera hosts a top 100 business podcast called *CEO School.*

> "Nothing bad happens when women make more money."

My Five Wisdoms

1. "Family" first.

In our culture, family always comes first. "Family" includes neighbors and nonrelatives; we treat everyone like family. That welcoming, hospitable nature instilled in me naturally carried over into my leadership style and our company's values. "One team, one dream" is truly how we operate, where everyone—emploees, customers, and vendors—are part of our Stax extended family in a meaningful way.

2. Maintain an abundance mindset.

These days, people talk about having an abundance mindset, but this perspective is core to my immigrant culture. Whatever we had, even if it wasn't much, wasn't just enough; it was more than enough. So, we never grew up with a scarcity mindset and were always grateful for everything we had. This abundance mindset has catapulted our business because I see endless opportunities.

3. A strong work ethic.

My parents didn't go to college, so entrepreneurship was necessary, not something cool they dabbled in. Growing up in that entrepreneurial environment, I observed an immense work ethic. I learned that no job was too big or small, regardless of your age. I saw my parents do it all, not afraid of working hard. It inspired me to put in the work, day in and day out, to build our company.

4. Respect others.

I was raised to treat people with dignity and respect, always say hi, hold doors open, and offer guests a glass of water. There was a level of kindness for everyone. That emphasis on respecting humankind made me a better leader. As an immigrant kid, those leadership skills helped me naturally find ways to interact with people at all different levels, care for them, and make them feel important.

5. Create joy.

Growing up, we didn't have much. It didn't mean we couldn't have fun. We spent so much quality time together, focusing on experiences that created joy. My house was always filled with laughter and good times, which is true for most immigrant families. That value was a huge part of how I grew up and is embedded in our company culture, team environment, and creating joy for our customers.

JODIE W. McLEAN

CEO, EDENS

Jodie W. McLean is Chief Executive Officer of EDENS, one of the nation's leading private owners, operators, and developers of retail real estate. For over 25 years, she has been a critical player in EDENS's growth and expansion to its current marketplace leadership, capitalized by blue chip investors and assets valued at $6.5 billion. Jodie serves on several boards, including Cushman & Wakefield (NYSE: CWK), the Federal Reserve Bank of Richmond, Milhaus Multi-Family, Mashburn, and Wofford College. She is also a Trustee of ICSC, the Urban Land Institute (ULI), and The Real Estate Roundtable. Jodie is a member of the Liberty Fellowship (Aspen Institute), Class of 2009.

> "Take the shot! Put yourself in the arena and take risks. If you don't, you will never know your own potential. If you fail, dust yourself off and try again."

My Five Wisdoms

1. Find the right partners at work and in life.
Choose those with whom your values align and who will both support you and share radical candor with you.

2. Align with institutions that have a clear sense of purpose.
Select organizations that align with your own values. It will accelerate your personal and professional success.

3. Be willing to break things.
The status quo is not sacred. The comfort found within the herd cannot rival the thrill of leading. And remember, sometimes the most courageous form of leadership is to be the first follower.

4. Find comfort in your discomfort.
Step into the arena, work hard, and listen even harder. Make a mistake every single day because that is where growth comes from. If you aren't making mistakes and stubbing your toe, you aren't learning and you're living in a zone of mediocrity. Excellence lives outside your comfort zone.

5. And never forget that kindness is the most underrated value in business.
Kindness will lead to greater team stability, creativity, and innovation.

PHYLLIS NEWHOUSE

CEO AND FOUNDER, SHOULDERUP TECHNOLOGY ACQUISITION CORP.

Phyllis Newhouse is a serial entrepreneur, investor, retired military senior officer, and mentor. She is CEO and Founder of ShoulderUp Technology Acquisition Corp., Founder and CEO of Xtreme Solutions, Inc. (XSI), CEO of Athena Technology Acquisition Corp., and Founder of ShoulderUp, a 501(c)(3). As a pioneer in cybersecurity and business, Phyllis is the first woman to win an EY Entrepreneur of the Year award in the technology category. She is also the first African American female CEO to take a SPAC public. Phyllis's leadership and business success have been featured in *Today, Entrepreneur, Inc.,* CNBC, *Forbes,* Yahoo! Finance, Cheddar News, Bloomberg, and more.

> "People are most intrigued by who you are, not what you do. The next time you walk into a room, remember to lead with WHO you are because it's the key to making more powerful and meaningful connections."

My Five Wisdoms

1. Leverage your ROCs: Resources, Opportunities, Connections.

We all carry a bag of ROCs daily. Learn to support others by giving them resources, opportunities, and connections. Know what ROCs you're looking for, and don't be afraid to ask for them. The more you learn to give away, the more you receive.

2. "Support," not "help."

Not everyone wants to give and receive help. However, the connotation changes when you change your terminology from "help" to "support." Everyone loves to give and receive support. Ask "How can I support you?" and see what a difference it makes!

3. Know your value card.

Each of us has a value card. It's what you're world-class at. Mine is leadership and negotiation. When I walk into a room, I know I can play my value card in a way where no one else can beat me. Your value card makes you unstoppable. Know yours and know when to play it.

4. WED = Win Every Day

I make every day a winning day by concentrating on my wins, however small. Don't forget to celebrate wins. Closed a client? Celebrate! Did you get to work early and finish your day's main priority? Celebrate! You'll quickly realize that celebrating and accomplishing small wins conditions you to anticipate bigger ones, and small wins stack. That's why I say EVERY DAY is a winning day!

5. The Three Ds: Detours, Distractions, and Disappointment

Our journeys are filled with these three Ds. When faced with an obstacle, know what you're going up against. If it's a distraction, ignore it. If it's a disappointment, take your time to grieve, but not too long. Then move on. If it's a detour, find an alternative solution. Success is about diagnosing which one of the three Ds you're up against and taking the appropriate path to handle it.

CAROL B. TOMÉ

CEO, UPS

Carol B. Tomé became Chief Executive Officer of UPS in June 2020.
Previously, she served as Executive Vice President and Chief Financial Officer of The Home Depot, Inc. Carol is a Board Member for Verizon Communications, Inc., and a Trustee for Grady Memorial Hospital Corporation and the Atlanta Botanical Garden. She is also President of the Tomé Foundation and a member of several civic and business councils. A native of Jackson, Wyoming, Carol holds a bachelor's degree in communication from the University of Wyoming and an MBA in finance from the University of Denver.

> "Don't make money your goal. Instead, pursue the things you love doing and do them so well that people can't take their eyes off you."
> —Maya Angelou

My Five Wisdoms

1. Invest in your physical and emotional well-being.

I have a personal trainer, and I work out with her three times a week. I also have a personal coach and speak with her two times a month. I've learned that it is impossible to lead effectively, nurture and develop a team . . . or in other words, "care for a team," until I first care for myself. This focus isn't selfish. It is self-preservation.

2. Remember that leadership is action and not position.

Don't measure your success by title. Measure it by impact.

3. Declare your personal purpose statement.

It will guide your actions and lead to a more fulfilling life. My purpose is to Lead to Inspire, Serve to Create, and Give to Remain. If you have listened to Hamilton, you may remember this lyric written by Lin-Manuel Miranda. It goes: "When you are gone . . . who remembers your name . . . who keeps your flame . . . who tells your story?" Your story will be told by your purpose.

4. Lean into your career.

But know that if you are leaning in, you are leaning away from something (it's just gravity). Make sure you are comfortable with what you are leaning away from and share that decision with others so they can support you.

5. Don't sweat the small stuff.

JUDITH M. VON SELDENECK

FOUNDER AND CHAIR, DIVERSIFIED SEARCH GROUP

Judith M. von Seldeneck is the Founder and Chair of Diversified Search Group. Judee founded Diversified Search in 1974 with the vision of finding professional roles for women and has built the company into one of the nation's top 10 executive search firms. She has served on numerous public and not-for-profit boards and received dozens of awards and honors recognizing her professional and philanthropic achievements, including the William Penn Award, the highest honor bestowed by the business community of Greater Philadelphia. Judee also founded the Forum of Executive Women, the largest association of women business leaders in the Philadelphia region, and recently created the JVS Philadelphia Fund for Women Entrepreneurs, providing funding for women-owned start-ups and early-stage companies.

> "Business success requires instincts and risk-taking, but it's also about respect, teamwork, collaboration, and sharing in prosperity. Understanding this has enabled us to have the success we have had."

My Five Wisdoms

1. Be forward-thinking and keep your finger on the pulse of what's coming next.
History and experience are great teachers, but there is great value and potential in what new generations have to offer. The workforce is more diverse than ever. Learn to connect with and listen to people from all backgrounds and walks of life.

2. Recognize those who have helped you along the way, and be generous in sharing your success.
Nearly 50 years ago, women entrepreneurs faced limited access to capital. While I am pleased to see that changing, I felt fortunate to create the JVS Philadelphia Fund for Women Entrepreneurs, providing women-led enterprises with a source of capital for business growth.

3. Be willing to make sacrifices and make tough decisions.
Success in the business world comes at a price, and it's not for everyone. You must make sacrifices and difficult decisions to balance your quality of life. I've started a company, sold it, repurchased it, and found new investors. Ultimately, you must believe in yourself and recognize that you need others to wish you well if you're going to succeed.

4. First impressions matter.
Most people are quick to judge others, so how you present yourself matters. Your persona and how you communicate are key. Be authentic and transparent, and show genuine interest in others. You need to make the connection, and often you only have one shot at it.

5. Enjoy life. Time is short and valuable.
It is easy to say, "Eliminate stress from your life," but it comes with the territory, and you need to know how to manage it. Change is inevitable, and I've learned that nothing lasts forever, good or bad. One of the most gratifying and fulfilling things for me is that we were able to create a culture at Diversified Search Group that has been like family. We work hard, we play hard, and we treasure our time together.

"Be a beacon of light and hope. . . . Channel the voices of the unseated on the board, and with their voices, there can be positive change."

—Paula A. Price

CHAPTER 2

WOMEN ON BOARDS:
CELEBRATING BUSINESS CHAMPIONS

The women in this chapter sit on the boards of some of the largest domestic and international corporations. And yet they are collectively dismayed at how difficult it has been in the past to be elected or selected for a corporate board.

Today, getting more women and women of diverse backgrounds on these boards is happening because boards recognize that women are valuable assets to their organizations. But it has taken great effort and at times political mandates to move women onto those board seats.

Boards are the gatekeepers of governance, strategy, purpose, and impact. A growing body of research suggests that corporate performance is stronger when there is a significant proportion of women on the boards of a company. Women improve the decision making and board efficiency, and the data suggest there are fewer financial restatements, fewer governance-related issues, and improved brand reputation.

Remember, the most critical role of a corporate board is to provide strategic oversight for a company. Imagine being a woman who can now influence another company's growth and values because the board members embrace her perspectives.

The women in this chapter will tell you that bringing a diverse perspective is needed to thrive in these fast-changing times. But for you, read about why you should never second-guess your capabilities. Rather, you should feel the power of being "uncomfortably excited." Reflect on the generous spirit of their wisdom so that you, too, can become part of the transformation on corporate boards that is taking place today for a better future.

These women are pushing forward the front lines of change and have broken into challenging places. They show up, and they mean business.

SHELLYE ARCHAMBEAU

**FORTUNE 500 BOARD MEMBER;
FORMER CEO, METRICSTREAM;
ADVISOR AND AUTHOR**

———————

Shellye Archambeau is an experienced CEO and board director building brands, high-performance teams, and organizations. She currently serves on the boards of Verizon, Roper Technologies, and Okta. She is also a strategic advisor to Forbes Ignite and the President of Arizona State University, and Shellye serves on the board of two national nonprofits, Catalyst and Braven. With over 30 experienced years in technology, she is the former CEO of MetricStream, a Silicon Valley–based governance, risk, and compliance software company. She grew MetricStream from a fledgling start-up into a global market leader. She is the author of *Unapologetically Ambitious: Take Risks, Break Barriers, and Create Success on Your Own Terms,* a *Forbes* contributor, and the protagonist of the Harvard Business School Case Study "Shellye Archambeau: Becoming a CEO."

> "Most people have more power than they think they have. The most significant power you have is your voice. Use your voice to ask for help and what you need in life and at work. Asking for help is a strength, not a weakness."

My Five Wisdoms

1. Be intentional so you can achieve your aspirations.

"Growing up, as a little Black girl in the U.S., I didn't feel seen or valued. I learned that by setting goals and intentionally working toward them, I could improve my odds of achieving them. Challenges and hurdles become easier to navigate when you have the destination in mind."

2. Tell the universe what you want.

Stay unapologetically ambitious. Ask for what you need, and learn to let people help you. They can't support you on your journey if they don't know what you want. Just remember, no one achieves anything of significance all by themselves. Everyone needs help, so allow yourself to receive it.

3. Determine what needs to be true for your goals to happen.

When you set a goal, research to understand what others did to achieve the goal you set for yourself, then create a plan for yourself. Every organization has paths to power. I call these paths currents. Find the current to move forward faster. I was at IBM for 14 years, and my goal was to become CEO of IBM. I started in sales because every CEO at IBM began in sales. I jumped into the current.

4. Ambition and hard work alone aren't enough.

Homework does not stop at school. Research to figure out how to get what you want. Then create a plan to get there. The plan's power lies in making daily decisions consistent with the plan. That is how you stay on track to improve your odds of achieving your goals.

5. Treat people you admire as your mentors.

Mentoring relationships don't have to be formal. Just treat people you admire as mentors. Ask for their advice or perspective; in return, let them know how their counsel impacts you. Make sure you have many mentors. The more, the better. Mentors play huge roles. Very few of my mentoring relationships were formal. Yet their impact on me and my career was significant.

ANA DUTRA

GLOBAL CEO, BUSINESS ADVISOR, AND BOARD DIRECTOR

Ana Dutra is an experienced global CEO, business advisor, and board director of publicly traded family-owned and private corporations. A Latina with 30-plus years of experience in P&L management; environmental, social, and corporate governance; digital technology; and business growth in more than 25 countries, Ana is fluent in five languages. Ana led acquisitions, integrations, and joint ventures. As a CEO and P&L leader, she created $500 million businesses. Ana holds a Kellogg MBA, an MSEcon from Pontifical Catholic University of Rio de Janeiro, and a JD from Federal University of Rio de Janeiro. She received the Chicago United Business Leader of Color, Nueva Estrella Latina, and the SHEroes Role Model, among other awards. Ana, the bestselling author of *Lessons in LeadershiT,* is a proud mother of three daughters and an avid triathlete and yogini. Ana lives in Florida with her husband and their three dogs.

> "Nothing gives me more joy than paying it forward and helping others to achieve their goals and dreams."

My Five Wisdoms

1. Never second-guess your capabilities.
You are smart, driven, and creative. You can succeed in everything when you put your passion into it. When you second-guess your capabilities, remember, "You are seeing other people's outside with your inside!"

2. Your real job interview starts on your first day in any role.
Demonstrate your hard work, willingness to learn, and people skills, all the time. Be the First-In-Last-Out, even in Zoom meetings. Contrary to typical inventory accounting systems, F-I-L-O still wins the game in your career. Work ethics and self-awareness trump everything.

3. Observe the dynamics and unspoken rules of the team, workplace, and boardroom.
They are, sometimes, very different and more important than what is stated on paper. Learn, learn, learn beyond any task, no matter what you are doing. Learn about the culture, industry, organization, stakeholders, and relationship with them. Your role—no matter what it is—will suddenly become much more interesting.

4. No task is too small a task when you are representing your organization, team, or community.
That's the genuine STEWARDSHIP of any situation in life. Anticipate issues and opportunities and be proactive about addressing them. Always have a plan B. Everybody loves people who anticipate problems and tackle them before they become a reality.

5. Finally, have fun and enjoy the ride!
Make lifelong friends. Value relationships throughout your life. You will meet interesting people, travel around, and get to know new businesses and industries. Most of my former colleagues, team members, and peers became friends for life.

MARGO GEORGIADIS

SERIAL CEO; BOARD LEADER, MCDONALD'S, APPLOVIN, HANDSHAKE, CATALYST, C200

Margo Georgiadis is a serial CEO, investor, and public and private company board leader. Her passion for transforming products and services with data and technology empowers consumers to live better lives and delivers outsized returns for investors. She has served as the CEO of Montai Health/ Flagship Pioneering, Ancestry, and Mattel, as well as President, Americas at Google. She appeared on *Fortune*'s "50 Most Powerful Women in Business" list and received the *Forbes* "Excellence Award in Innovation" and is a dedicated champion of women as a company leader, board member (McDonald's, AppLovin, Handshake, Catalyst, C200), investor, and mentor to over 25 women founders/CEOs in technology and digital health.

> "Take risks to grow faster from opportunities that stretch and broaden your perspective and experience. Embrace the power of being 'uncomfortably excited.'"

My Five Wisdoms

1. Stay curious and inclusive.

A rapidly changing world driven by technological shifts, consumer expectations, global instability, and social and economic disparities requires leadership agility and adaptability. To refresh my perspectives, I try to meet three new people weekly in adjacent or emerging areas. I hold regular deep listening sessions across all levels of our organization—great ideas come from everywhere!

2. Demonstrate resilience and positivity.

How we face the inevitable ups and downs defines us as leaders. Learning to admit mistakes openly and fail forward fast creates energy and trust. People want to be around leaders that take ownership and lift them up. Positivity is a choice.

3. Create boundaries to stay centered.

As women, we can have it all, but often not all at once. As a wife, mom of three, parent caregiver, community volunteer, and business leader, finding time for myself is often challenging. Having kids early in my career forced me to set clear boundaries. I also started a practice for myself and teams of setting a personal goal alongside our business goals each quarter, "one simple thing." It's bonding to share and give each other permission to do what matters most.

4. Make your own luck.

An early mentor shared: "Successful people don't get lucky; they make their own luck." Ask yourself: Do I opt to stay in my comfort zone versus stretching myself? Am I passionate about what I'm doing to stay at peak energy? Do I work with people who challenge and help me create new opportunities? Put yourself in the path of opportunity.

5. Invest in a personal board of directors.

Building relationships early with a support team of peers, mentors, and sponsors—both women and men—helped me aim higher and go further. These advisors were pivotal in sharing direct and honest advice as well as the occasional "shove" when self-doubt or fears crept in at moments of transition. Now I love to be on personal boards to pay it forward!

HEIDI KLEINBACH-SAUTER

NON-EXECUTIVE DIRECTOR FOR CHR. HANSEN A/S
AND ROYAL UNIBREW A/S DENMARK

Heidi Kleinbach-Sauter is an innovative business, brand, and consumer-focused leader with an extensive track record of identifying, developing, and commercializing large, sustainable innovation platforms across many foods, beverages, and nonfood fast-moving consumer goods (FMCG) categories. She has deep, broad scientific and technical experience in more than 10 consumer goods categories and through her leadership has driven impressive business results. Her innovation responsibilities have spanned the U.S., Latin America, Western and Eastern Europe, the Middle East, Asia, and Australia. Her leadership and business experience range from small entrepreneurial family-owned companies to large global corporations. She last served as Senior Vice President of Global R&D at PepsiCo and currently serves as a Board Member at Chr. Hansen A/S Denmark and Royal Unibrew A/S Denmark. Heidi is actively engaged in supporting women to thrive in senior leadership positions. She serves as a member of the Board of Directors of the Women Business Collaborative and as a founding Chair and Cochair of STEMconnector, focusing on attracting young female talent into a STEM education. Heidi has been named one of "The Top 100 Women Leaders in STEM."

> "The most impactful career accelerator has been my family support system to help hold kids, our parents, and our family together. This support system is critical for every woman to be able to focus on the challenges of accelerating any career."

My Five Wisdoms

1. Be yourself and stay authentic.

Stay authentic, stay true to your values, speak your mind, believe in yourself, and be bold.

2. Build friendships, and use your power to influence.

Help other women accelerate their careers, and build friendships rather than networks. Walk the talk, and use your power to actively change HR processes and systems to drive equal pay, position, and power for women in business. Go deep, ask questions, drive key performance indicators, and do not accept the status quo until we have reached parity for women in business at all levels.

3. Stretch yourself and be bold.

Reach for the moon and the stars; do not stop going after the most daunting jobs. You will be amazed how much you can stretch and succeed big time. As you accelerate your career, ensure your family support system is solid and sustainable. Most senior jobs have limited space for work-life balance. If you do not have a support system to care for kids, parents, and family, it won't be easy to focus on your career. To refocus on you is probably one of the most underestimated issues as we progress in our careers.

4. Self-manage your career.

Please don't rely on others to progress in your career; proactively identify opportunities and go after them. Mentors give helpful directions, but you drive the car. Trust your gut. Follow your instincts.

5. Be open to change in every way.

Remain flexible and open to new learnings, new companies, new brands, new geographies, new bosses, and new challenges, and feel comfortable being thrown into cold waters.

ANTOINETTE "TONIE" LEATHERBERRY

BOARD MEMBER, ZOETIS, AMERICAN FAMILY INSURANCE, DIRECT DIGITAL HOLDINGS

Antoinette "Tonie" Leatherberry serves on the boards of Zoetis, American Family Insurance, and Direct Digital Holdings. A passionate and invested leader, Tonie retired from Deloitte in 2020. In addition to client responsibilities, she devoted much of her professional life to creating opportunities for women and people of color. She recently served as Chair of the Executive Leadership Council (ELC), a preeminent association of Black business leaders, focusing on board and executive leadership development, philanthropy, and talent development.

She has authored numerous articles and publications on information technology and governance and was named to the National Association of Corporate Directors (NACD) Directorship 100 in 2019 and 2020.

Tonie also serves on the Board of Trustees for Widener University and Boston University. She holds a bachelor's degree in mechanical engineering from Boston University and an MBA from Northeastern University and is currently pursuing a doctorate in higher education at Widener University.

> "Invest in others early and often. Great leaders cannot lead if there is no one to inspire, no stakeholders to influence, no ability to rise in the face of adversity, and no realization that the mission is bigger than them."

My Five Wisdoms

1. Develop and maintain the highest level of technical knowledge in your craft.
Be known as one of the top "go-to" people.

2. Know who the movers and shakers are.
Position yourself to be on their team. Make sure you are seen as someone willing to give more than you take and always offer to do so.

3. Know your business.
Understand the market and related trends, the competitive landscape, your organization's position for success, and your relevance in the market ecosystem. Always maintain a roadmap for success and solicit input from others on how to navigate.

4. Be passionate, and make your growth objectives known.
Passion shines through and is infectious. When others see this kind of energy, coupled with talent and ambition, they will be more eager to invest in your success. Once you have established your objectives, determine how to create a set of actions and milestones to drive success.

5. Mentoring is a two-way street.
Often, when people reach out for advice or ask someone to be their mentor, they tend to focus on what they will receive. Investing in that mentoring relationship and your mentor's success will go a long way to strengthening the connection.

SINGLETON McALLISTER

ATTORNEY, HUSCH BLACKWELL; CHAIR, CHART INDUSTRIES; BOARD MEMBER, ALLIANT ENERGY, ANTERIX, SECURITAS INFRASTRUCTURE SERVICES

Singleton McAllister is an attorney with Husch Blackwell. She has led a trailblazing legal career for over three decades in international relations and public policy law. She has served numerous public service appointments, including senior counsel to the House of Representatives Committee and on the Budget and General Counsel of USAID. Singleton has served on multiple corporate boards. She has been nationally recognized for her corporate leadership, including Women's Inc. Most Influential Corporate Directors and the National Association of Corporate Directors' Directorship 100. She holds a JD from Howard University School of Law and a BA from the University of Maryland. Elizabeth State University awarded Singleton an honorary doctorate.

> "Women should be represented in every aspect of our society. Serving on the Alliant Energy Board of Directors, I have witnessed that we are uniquely qualified for positions that men have traditionally occupied. Women are the engine that runs our economy."

My Five Wisdoms

1. Don't be afraid of personal insights.
Be willing to accept counsel from individuals with your best interests. Have a personal board of directors who can advise you on various issues affecting your life's journey.

2. "No" is a complete sentence.
Women inevitably want to please. We often overcommit ourselves to family, work, and outside activities. We perform as superwomen and need to understand our limitations better and take care of ourselves for what is essential in our lives.

3. Leave toxic people behind.
Have positive and nurturing people in your life—those you trust and value for their judgment and counsel.

4. Exercise is strong medicine.
Take time to maintain a fit body that will support a sound mind.

5. Don't take disagreements personally.
You may have a different opinion from others. However, it would be best if you attempted to understand their opinion without making it personal.

PAULA A. PRICE

INDEPENDENT BOARD DIRECTOR, ACCENTURE, BRISTOL MYERS SQUIBB, WARNER BROS. DISCOVERY

Paula A. Price is an Independent Board Director for Accenture, Bristol Myers Squibb, and Warner Bros. Discovery. She is also a strategic advisor/ director to pre-IPO, private, and nonprofit companies. She is the former Executive Vice President and Chief Financial Officer of Macy's, Inc., where she was a principal architect of its transformation journey and its financial restructuring during the COVID-19 pandemic.

Paula has also been Visiting Executive with Harvard Business School since July 2018 and, prior to that, was a full-time Senior Lecturer, having joined its faculty in 2014. Previously, she was Executive Vice President and Chief Financial Officer of Ahold USA and Controller and Chief Accounting Officer for CVS Health. A CPA, she earned her MBA from the University of Chicago and her BSc in accountancy from DePaul University.

> "Never be content with the accolades that come from being the 'only' or 'first.' Use your power to create space and extend a hand so that others may soon break through too."

My Five Wisdoms

1. Be a beacon of light and hope.

Corporate boardrooms are powerful spaces to help change the world for the better. Use your seat to channel the voices of the unseated. Bring their voices into the room repeatedly until there is a positive change.

2. Take time to get to know people across the organization.

You must be informed during succession planning, especially about women and untapped groups. Reach deep into the organization, and advocate for the developmental experiences they need to move up the ranks.

3. One of the greatest gifts we can give someone is to help them identify their "towering strength."

The skill that clearly distinguishes them from the next person is their towering strength. When someone is building out a team, someone else will say, "You need Ann on that team because she's really good at ___!" Please encourage them to own, hone, and leverage it to the hilt!

4. We need to hear your unique perspective in conversations around the big table.

Do not wait to find or perfect your voice, or you may miss the opportunity to have influence. Furthermore, one does not find one's voice. One develops it—by using it on issues that matter.

5. Be more visible.

This is a piece of, frankly, uncomfortable feedback that I once received that literally changed my trajectory by creating new opportunities. But, more importantly, by putting yourself out there, letting people hear and see YOU, saying "yes" to panels, conferences, fireside chats, etc., you may inspire someone else to be their best self.

MYRNA SOTO

BOARD MEMBER, PUBLICLY TRADED BOARDS: CMS ENERGY/ CONSUMERS ENERGY, SPIRIT AIRLINES, POPULAR, INC., (OPERATES AS BANCO POPULAR AND POPULAR BANK), TRINET. PRIVATE BOARDS: DELINEA, HEADSPACE HEALTH

Myrna Soto serves on the boards of CMS Energy/Consumers Energy, Spirit Airlines, TriNet, and Popular, Inc., which operates under the brand names of Banco Popular and Popular Bank. She is recognized as a Governance and Board Leadership Fellow by the National Association of Corporate Directors (NACD). In addition to her public board service, Myrna serves on the board of Delinea, a privately held cybersecurity technology provider, and the board of Headspace Health.

Myrna is also the Founder and CEO of Apogee Executive Advisors. Apogee Executive Advisors is a boutique advisory firm focused on providing strategic consulting in the areas of technology risk, cybersecurity, technology integrations, digital transformations, and enterprise risk management. She previously served as the Chief Strategy and Trust Officer for Forcepoint. Myrna also served as Chief Operating Officer of an award-winning Managed Security Service Provider (MSSP) and Managed Technology Services provider. Myrna was also an Investment Partner at Forgepoint Capital. Before the roles described above, Myrna served as Corporate Senior Vice President and Global Chief Information Security Officer for Comcast Corp. Prior to joining Comcast, Myrna served as CISO and Vice President of Information Technology Governance for MGM Resorts International.

> "I have made it my mantra never to be comfortable, and I am constantly stretching my limits and reaching for what may be 'next.'"

My Five Wisdoms

1. We are often told that it's all about work-life balance. However, in our careers, it is about work-life choices.
You can have everything you want, a great career, family, and all that comes with what many women want in life. The key is choice and timing. We can have it all, but it may not be possible all at the same time.

2. Women are often the center of support.
Never overlook the importance of the support system around you. The pillars we stand on and the discrete actions of those who love us mean a great deal to our ability to strive. Never forget who they are, what they have done, and how you represent success for them.

3. Never settle!
Throughout my career, I spent many years questioning the status quo and challenging what should be equitable. We often can set our limits and challenge ourselves. The job offer is good. Make the offer GREAT. You may not have every qualification for your dream job, but go for it anyway. You won't be disappointed.

4. Comfort is death.
If you find yourself comfortable, then it is time to change. Strive for constant learning; strive for change and continuous evolution. Live a life of continual curiosity and questioning.

5. For those women who have had a remarkable career and find themselves at a crossroads at a particular time of their lives, it is never OVER.
Reinventing yourself and creating the next chapter of your career is extremely fulfilling. We all go down traditional paths. Liberate yourself to explore the next chapter of your life with a new profession, a new track, or reinventing your experience. Retirement is a "rewirement."

"Use your listening skills to deepen connections and bring resolution to conflict."

—Sherlaender "Lani" Phillips

CHAPTER 3

CORPORATE EXECUTIVES AND LEADERS EXPANDING OPPORTUNITIES IN THE C-SUITE

Today, in businesses, women oversee all corporate functions, from operations to finance, marketing to human resources, technology to chief revenue officer, and everything in between. Women have roles in what were traditionally viewed as the male domain. In the past, these were difficult positions for women to access. Now, as women are being recruited and developed, they are diversifying the C-suite.

These corporate executives and leaders share the "big ideas" that were essential to their success. Looking back on their careers, they provide insights and reflections that will surprise you, even challenge you.

One woman's father's wisdom changed her career path. His work ethic became her rulebook for work and success in life. Another woman reminds you that we all need to hustle because there are always people who are smarter than you, more creative, and even luckier than you. Only you can control how hard you work. As you hustle, bring your true self to work, and see where it takes you on your journey.

Reaching their positions in business has not been easy. Now these women are in a place to better bring their experiences to help accelerate the growth of their companies and to help other women moving upward in their careers.

The proportion of women in senior executive roles globally has wonderful opportunities to expand. The women in this chapter will not stay silent as others join them to make a difference. The net result will increase the number of women in leadership roles, creating fuller gender parity and diversity in the C-suite.

Embrace the wisdom of these corporate executives and leaders to move yourself forward and blaze your own trail. As one of our amazing women urges us to repeat, "Be seen, be heard, and be recognized."

ASTER ANGAGAW

VICE PRESIDENT, HEAD OF COMMERCIAL, PUBLIC, AND STRATEGIC SECTORS, AMAZON BUSINESS WORLDWIDE

Aster Angagaw joined Amazon in January of 2022 and currently serves as the Vice President for Commercial, Public, and Strategic Sectors for Amazon Business Worldwide. Before joining Amazon, Aster served as President of ServiceMaster Brands. Before ServiceMaster, she served in a series of senior executive roles, culminating as the CEO of Healthcare North America at Sodexo SA, a Paris-headquartered multinational diversified services company. Prior to joining Amazon, Aster served on the boards of Owens & Minor, a leading Fortune 500 health care services company, and served on the board of Lucid Diagnostics, a commercial-stage cancer diagnostic company.

> "When you feel tired, look back and see how far you have come. When you feel complacent, look ahead and see how much is left to do."

My Five Wisdoms

1. Know you can be so much more.
Be good, do good, and go beyond wherever you are today. Go with faith that you can become whatever you dream of being. Make sure that "growth" is one of your daily deliverables, and ask what you will grow today.

2. Know you have a multidimensional life.
As I discuss in my book, as women, we need to be mindful and intentional in seven different areas of our lives, leveraging what I call the Seven Dimension Framework. What are your focus areas? Make sure it includes a career, your growth, the community, self-care, money, play, and purpose. Most of all, begin with your purpose; the rest will flow from what matters to you. Map out your life and think intentionally about what comes next for you. How are you structured, organized, and finding fulfillment?

3. Be very intentional about who you choose as a life partner.
Your choice can be your accelerator, inspiration, or anchor, dragging you backward. The power of that relationship can lead to deeper insights, a clear purpose, and great pleasure.

Don't underestimate how the time and ideas shared help you frame your life.

4. Embrace lopsidedness.
Your life will not always feel "in balance." Every day, we make choices, and it is not easy, but the tension is a positive opportunity to propel you forward. The idea of balance creates an illusion that all is well when it stops you from seeing what is possible. Think about integrating the different areas of your life and look for opportunities that fulfill several dimensions at once.

5. Periodically check in with yourself.
Make sure you are on track. You cannot predict the future, but you certainly can plan and prepare for it. Be curious and assume positive intent. You are on your way, and the future is yours to create. What you imagine persists.

CRYSTAL E. ASHBY

EXECUTIVE VICE PRESIDENT, IBX

Crystal E. Ashby is a nationally recognized leader with 30 years of experience developing talent, advancing inclusive workplace cultures, and building people-focused organizations. Her distinguished career includes executive positions in health care, energy, and nonprofit, including her current role as Executive Vice President and Chief People Officer for Independence Health Group (IBX). Crystal also served as interim President and Chief Executive Officer of The Executive Leadership Council.

Crystal has received accolades, including the No. 1 ranking in the City & State Pennsylvania Impact 50, *Savoy* Most Influential Black Executives in America, National Diversity Council Top 100 HR Professionals, Diversity Global Top 10 Influential Women in Diversity, and Uptown Professional Top 100 Executives in America. Her extensive board service includes positions with BAE Systems plc, Texas Reliability Entity, Inc., and her alma mater, the University of Michigan. Crystal is a member of the International Women's Forum and the American Bar Association.

> "Taking a risk is an opportunity to grow. You don't yet know everything you're capable of doing, and you never will unless you step out of your comfort zone."

My Five Wisdoms

1. Own your own self.

We spend too much time focusing on what others think. Spend that time looking inside yourself instead. Think, "How do I feel about this?" or "What do I need to do now?" More often than not, you know the answer. My grandmother used to say, "What other people think of you is none of your business."

2. Plans are great; opportunities are better.

Life is not a straight line—it's a series of curves, hills, and valleys. Make a plan, but lean into change and opportunity as they come. If plan A doesn't work, there's plan B; if plan Z has problems, there's plan A1. And even when a plan works, sometimes it's time to say, "That was amazing, but I'm ready to do something else." This can be tricky (I know; I'm a planner), but your best life might be just around the corner.

3. When you open new spaces, bring others into them.

The great things we achieve, we don't achieve by ourselves. Recognize whose shoulders you stand on, and pay them back by offering a shoulder to someone else. As you access new spaces, open them up to the people behind you. If you don't, those spaces will close up again.

4. Approach every relationship with care.

We never fully know the impact we're having on others. Make no presumptions or assumptions, but rather be open and give people the time they deserve. If you choose to be a friend, be a real friend. If you decide to be a mentor, understand what that means. You may find yourself with a new member of your board of directors.

5. Live life with no regrets.

We all face life changes, miss out on opportunities, and make mistakes. Know that everything happens for a reason, so learn from it. At the same time, if there is something you know you want, don't leave it to chance—you must actively pursue it. Importantly, that also includes deciding what else you CAN'T, don't, or won't do and being OK with some windows closing.

KIM BRINK

CHIEF REVENUE OFFICER, ELECTRAMECCANICA

Kim Brink is the Chief Revenue Officer of ElectraMeccanica. She is a strategist with public and private board experience. As a native Detroiter, Kim has spent her career untapping the power of the world's most iconic brands, including Chevrolet, Cadillac, Ford, and NASCAR. Kim has served on the boards of Arctic Cat, DealerSocket, and the Country Music Association. As the Chief Revenue Officer of ElectraMeccanica, Kim is helping build an innovative electric vehicle OEM (original equipment manufacturer) that designs purpose-built vehicles for today's modern buyers. Her greatest joys are her two Clemson Tigers, Stephen and Biz, and when she is not building brands, you will find her at the barn riding her quarter horse.

> "'Never give up!' —Louis Chevrolet
> "Not every day will be easy, so choose not to give up. Thanks, Chevy GM Jim Perkins, the intimidating Texan with a heart of gold, for sharing that with me many years ago."

My Five Wisdoms

1. If it doesn't feel right, it probably isn't.
Always trust your gut.

2. "I don't understand" can be mighty words.
Never be afraid to ask "why" or what all the acronyms mean that people may use. You can't contribute if you don't understand.

3. Show up on time; show up prepared.
Showing up on time means you respect others' time as much as your own. Showing up late sends the opposite signal. Show up prepared to make the most of your time and get the best results.

4. Set boundaries.
Identify the most important things to you and protect the boundaries around those things.

5. The most unexpected people will show up later to help you.
Always remember that.

LISA EDWARDS

EXECUTIVE CHAIR, DILIGENT INSTITUTE

Lisa Edwards is Executive Chair of Diligent Institute, the leading gover-nance, risk, and compliance SAAS provider, with more than $500 million in revenue. Lisa is responsible for commercial growth and performance. Prior to Diligent, she was Executive Vice President of Strategic Business Operations at Salesforce, after serving as Executive Vice President of Global Corporate Services. Lisa also held leadership positions at Visa, Inc., and KnowledgeX and cofounded ValuBond, before the company's acquisition by Knight Capital.

Lisa received a bachelor's degree from Stanford University and an MBA from Harvard Business School. She serves on the Board of Directors of Colgate-Palmolive Company.

> **"Hustle matters. People out there are smarter than you, more creative, and even luckier than you. You can only control how hard you work."**

My Five Wisdoms

1. Work for people you think you can learn from.

I've deliberately chosen to work for people I can learn from throughout my career. Managers matter, too, because you learn management by being managed. You understand what motivates versus disintegrates. Sometimes taking or staying in a suboptimal job is worthwhile if you are learning and building your skills.

2. Lead by example.

I'm incredibly passionate about giving women exposure—if they don't ever see what strong female leadership looks like, it's much harder for them to be strong leaders themselves. It is important to be visible. Don't hide your kids and talk about your obligations outside the office. We all have lives to balance.

3. Break down barriers to leadership with early intervention.

In the U.S., the proportion of women graduating from college is at 60 percent. We should see a workforce and leadership team that skews toward women. However, women only make up a small percent of the technology workforce and corporate leadership. We don't see women graduating with technical degrees going into tech companies. If we are going to move the needle, we should have early interventions to ensure girls are excited about math and science and to nurture that interest at a young age.

4. What gets measured gets managed.

To quote a friend, "If you think you have a pipeline problem, you may be looking down the wrong pipe." In addition to the education and access issues noted above, companies must attract and retain women.

5. Find your tribe and your support network.

To grossly oversimplify, men are historically better at networking than most women. They have a cadre of people they can call—for advice, for that next job, for a reference to an employment lawyer or a recruiter. Sometimes, women view after-work drinks or a golf game after a conference as a stolen moment. If you reframe these events as investing in building relationships, they become less optional.

And speaking of building relationships, choose your life partner wisely. Almost every successful woman I know either has a partner who supports and celebrates them or has taken on half (or well over half) of the child-rearing and household obligations and clears the runway for them.

LAKSHMI ELESWARPU

GLOBAL CIO

Lakshmi Eleswarpu is a technology executive leading enterprise strategies and digital transformation on a global scale at the world's leading companies, with a career spanning Boeing, HP, British-Telecom, Coca-Cola, and Procter & Gamble. As CIO, Lakshmi leads strategic initiatives on revenue growth, operating income, technology investments, cybersecurity, business transformation, supply chain, manufacturing, and consumer experience. Lakshmi is an electrical engineer from the University of Akron, Ohio.

> "Leadership is inspiring others to achieve their dreams. Passion is a fire burning to live a life of purpose, improving lives and changing the world."

My Five Wisdoms

1. Integrity, values, kindness, and respect.
Never compromise, whether it be how you treat others or how they treat you.

2. Bring the real you to everything you do.
Be proud of your identity and heritage. Keep what makes you special to your heart, and do not let anyone take it away from you. Influence decisions and others with your unique ideas. Individuality and passion combine for impactful leadership.

3. Rise to the challenges.
Focus on delivering with excellence. Take the time to learn and be the best self you can be. All good things will follow at each stage of your career.

4. Believe in yourself.
Humility is what makes you prepared, and confidence is what makes you execute successfully.

5. Courage is being able to stand and speak up when you see injustice.
Courage is being willing to sit down, listen to others, and take action to improve lives.

MICHELLE GADSDEN-WILLIAMS

MANAGING DIRECTOR AND GLOBAL HEAD OF DIVERSITY, EQUITY, AND INCLUSION (DEI), BLACKROCK

Michelle Gadsden-Williams is the Managing Director and Global Head of Diversity, Equity, and Inclusion (DEI) for BlackRock, the world's largest asset management firm. She is an award-winning global diversity executive, author, activist, and philanthropist with more than 25 years of experience as an advocate for equality within corporate America.

Michelle earned a BS in marketing and a BA in communications from Kean College of New Jersey and an MS in organizational dynamics from the University of Pennsylvania. She also has an honorary doctor of humane letters degree from Kean University for her outstanding personal and professional accomplishments in the field of DEI.

> "We are not here on this earth to occupy space. We are here to make a difference. It is up to us to determine what that difference is."
>
> — Michelle's father, Herbert Gadsden, Jr.

My Five Wisdoms

1. Ask for what you want and what you deserve.

Research has shown that one of the many reasons why women often don't get what they want (and deserve) is because there is a reluctance to ask for it. Men are more likely than women to negotiate for what they want. These same studies have also shown that women aren't bad at negotiating. We're simply bad at negotiating for ourselves. Women, do one thing—choose courage over comfort. Ask for what you want without fear. When that inner voice tells you that you're not smart enough, you don't have enough experience, or that you don't check every box, ask anyway!

2. There's no place for imposter syndrome or self-doubt.

Women fall prey to this idea of imposter syndrome when they doubt their abilities. For women of color, this feeling of self-doubt is often more pronounced. I have not experienced this in my career. I may have felt uncertain. Take the time to find role models who consistently demonstrate their courage and conviction.

3. Flying stealth (or below the radar) is not an option.

Keeping your head down or "flying stealth" is not what will get you noticed on the job and certainly won't get you promoted. Raising your hand for challenging assignments, doing the extras, and fostering meaningful relationships is key!

4. Leverage your uniqueness and experiences as teachable moments.

I revel in my "otherness" as a woman of color. My experiences are different, and my climb up the corporate ladder is not the same as some of my colleagues. It is incumbent upon each of us to treat others with dignity, mutual respect, and understanding.

5. Intention extends far beyond having ambition.

"Intentionality" is one of my favorite words. No matter what company or industry I've worked in, my intention has always been clear—and that is to leave a company in better condition than when I arrived. Success begins and ends with YOU!

CINDY KENT

COO, EVERLY HEALTH

Cindy Kent is a health care executive and corporate director recognized for her transformational leadership. Cindy is the Chief Operating Officer at Everly Health—the digital health company at the forefront of the diagnostics industry. Before Everly Health, Cindy was the Executive Vice President and President of Senior Living Community Operations for Brookdale Senior Living and had executive roles at 3M, Medtronic, and Eli Lilly.

Cindy is an Independent Director for Accolade and a Nomination and Governance Committee member. She was also a member of Best Buy Co.'s Board of Directors from 2018 to 2020. Cindy is currently a Trustee of Vanderbilt University.

Recognized for her commitment to excellence in the workplace and community, *Directors & Boards* named Cindy a "Director to Watch" in its August 2021 magazine. In its spring 2020 edition, *Savoy Magazine* named Cindy one of the "Most Influential Black Executives in Corporate America." In 2017, *Black Enterprise* magazine named her one of the "Top 100 Most Powerful Women in Business" and one of the "Most Powerful Executives in Corporate America." Cindy was recognized as one of the "Top 35 Women Leaders in Healthcare" by the Women's Health Leadership TRUST in 2014. She is a Henry Crown Fellow of the Aspen Institute.

> "Our deepest fear is not that we are inadequate. Our deepest fear is that we are powerful beyond measure . . ."
>
> —Marianne Williamson

My Five Wisdoms

1. Leave a legacy.

It is never too early to consider the legacy we want to leave in the world. One of my personal mantras is "Leave people, places, and things better than I find them." Ask: "What is my impact here?" You want to look back and see how your efforts mattered in the lives of others.

2. Mentors and sponsors are critically important.

As I began my career, I had little idea what a great sponsor could provide me. I had learned about mentors, but women are over-mentored and under-sponsored. One senior executive saw something in me far beyond what I knew I could become. His direct support proved to be a catalytic moment in my career journey. He taught me the power of sponsorship. How are you a mentor or a sponsor?

3. Ask for help.

Whether your support system is formal or informal, it is important to surround yourself with people who can listen to your ideas and offer advice. It is OK to say, "I don't know," but challenge yourself to find the answers through your teams and others. We need people whose experiences we can tap into when the answers are not obvious.

4. Find your own soul joy.

You might ask, what is "soul joy"? One of my best friends used to ask, "Is your soul still singing?" When my answer was no, we'd have a deeper conversation about what was getting in the way. I call this sentiment soul joy. Is your soul singing? What brings you pleasure and purpose?

5. Be fearless.

I learned a valuable lesson about fearlessness years ago. I was with childhood friends when one called me fearless, and I was struck by her assessment. We'd known each other since we were teens and shared many life moments. When I challenged her description, her response was an "aha" moment. "Yes," she said, "but you never let those fears stop you."

JILL MARCOTTE

PARTNER, CHIEF SUPPLY CHAIN OFFICER, DEALER TIRE

Jill Marcotte is Partner/Part Owner of the Dealer Tire enterprise of companies totaling over $3 billion. Jill helped create the overall corporate strategic and tactical foundation for the highly successful wholesale distribution company that Dealer Tire has become. As part of her executive role, Jill serves as the Board Chair of the enterprise's strategic investment, Simple Tire. Jill also serves on two private boards, and Jill was previously named "Director to Watch," "Inspirational Women in Supply Chain," and "Woman to Watch in the Tire Industry." Jill has previously held leadership roles at Brach's Confections, Andes Candies, Nestlé, and General Motors.

> "Know yourself. Know what fuels you. Know your superpower. Embrace/leverage it. Love what you do. Touch, move, and inspire others to be their best version of themselves."

My Five Wisdoms

1. Relentlessly be available for other women.

Encourage and support women to pursue their ambitions and succeed in their professional endeavors. Put in the time to move mountains to help women achieve greatness. Encourage girls early in life to think big and have confidence in themselves. Start close to home. I have impacted my two nieces' choices to go into supply chain and engineering due to my encouragement and support. I advocate for diversity on boards and have helped several women get their first director position.

2. Take risks, and venture into unknown territory. Power through!

Be adventurous. Build bridges for future women. Enter and expand in male-dominated industries/roles. Remember, any hurdle or difficulty is temporary. Champion your self-acceptance, confidence, and the power to act. Years ago, I earned a bachelor's and master's in engineering. I started my professional career at an automotive forging parts plant in Detroit, pushing the envelope of acceptance of women in new places.

3. Clearly understand your inherent strengths, and match your career to leverage those strengths.

Let your assets guide your path. Find opportunities where your strengths can propel the organization. Have a voice so that when you speak, people listen. Read the room. I find that my balance of operational and strategic strengths combined with my ability to build associate-engaging solid cultures are best suited for building and supporting large companies with complex growth plans.

4. Create exceptional workplaces by driving inclusive and engaging cultures.

Join companies that have great cultures. Continue to build a welcoming, fulfilling workplace. At Dealer Tire, I have been part of the partner group that created an open, engaging culture through our core values of fairness, accountability, innovation, and playing to win. We encourage a culture that feels like family.

5. Build long-lasting memories.

We have limited time to be everything to everyone. Find ways to create unforgettable memories with the people close to you. As the working parent in our family, I created memorable trips and photo books with those closest to me. Those excursions became vivid memories for those special people in my life.

JENNIFER McCOLLUM

CEO, LINKAGE, INC. (A SHRM COMPANY)

Jennifer McCollum is CEO of Linkage, a 35-year-old leadership development firm with a mission to "Change the Face of Leadership." Linkage works with organizations globally to advance women and accelerate inclusion in leaders and organizations. Jennifer is also an author, keynote speaker, and consultant and has been building and leading businesses in the leadership space for more than 20 years. Her expertise includes the state of women in the workforce, how to close the gap in gender equity, why the most influential leaders are inclusive leaders, and how to demystify inclusion for leaders and organizations.

> "Invite the work that aligns with your passion and strength. You don't have to prove yourself in all things. Free yourself to say no."

My Five Wisdoms

1. Envision the leader you want to become, and focus your energy there.

Getting clarity on who you are—your calling, values, and dreams—makes it possible to align your time and resources to your greatest aspiration. Women are often told to seize every opportunity, which can leave us exhausted. We don't need to prove our value by over-rowing the boat. Take your foot off the gas a bit and empower others to help. Doing less work allows you to do your best work in the areas most meaningful to you.

2. Become a friend and coach to your inner critic.

We all have a voice in our head that tears us down; instills shame, doubt, or fear; and prevents us from taking bold action. That same inner critic can also drive us to judge others. We can't silence the voice, but we can calm it and stop letting it control our behaviors. We can pause, find compassion for ourselves and others, and act from there.

3. Surround yourself with people who support you and lift you.

Who is your tribe? Make a sincere effort to find your people and spend more time with them. Be vulnerable with them. Reach out to them when you're feeling lost or needing help. The people who care about you most see your value more clearly than you do. They will also help build your confidence so others can see it, too.

4. Ensure that others recognize your greatness and authenticity.

Women have spent too much time contorting into an outdated image of traditional leadership. We have stayed small, worked hard, and hoped others would notice. It's time to embrace and promote our brand and accomplishments so others recognize us for who we truly are and honor who we are becoming.

5. Lift others as you rise.

We have the privilege and responsibility to help other women as we advance in our leadership. Find ways to be a sponsor or mentor the next generation of powerful women. Show them the way forward—open doors to your network and opportunities. Women have strength and power in greater numbers than ever before. It benefits all of us to help any of us.

MIA MENDS

CEO, C&W SERVICES, A DIVISION OF
CUSHMAN & WAKEFIELD

Mia Mends spent a decade in senior leadership roles at Sodexo, including Global Chief Diversity, Equity & Inclusion Officer, serving as Chief Administrative Officer (CAO) of North America, and designing an integrated target operating model for the $10 billion business while leading 160,000 employees. She also served as CEO of Impact Ventures, which included SodexoMagic, a joint venture between Sodexo and Magic Johnson Enterprise.

Mia serves on the Board of Directors for the EMERGE Fellows program and the Business Leadership Council at Wellesley College and is a corporate director at H&R Block and Limeade, Inc. Mia holds an MBA from Harvard Business School and a bachelor's degree in economics from Wellesley College and was named by *Black Enterprise* as one of the Most Powerful Women in Corporate America.

> "Leadership is about service. In ascending to a leadership role, you must cultivate a servant's heart and understand that leadership is an act of selflessness. Our role is to serve the mission and people."

My Five Wisdoms

1. A meaningful career requires persistence and grit.

Persevering through the complex and ugly produces greatness and joy. I have embraced the all-too-human path marked by setbacks, derailments, and disappointments. Setbacks are essential ingredients in wisdom and resilience. If there is no struggle, there is no progress.

2. My life journey is anchored in humanity and authenticity.

I choose to be kind, compassionate, humble, and even vulnerable. All this comes from enduring and learning under challenging times. When you are open and vulnerable with others, it permits them to do the same. This vulnerability helps to create high-performing teams.

3. Bring women along, and give them the support they deserve.

I stand on the shoulders of incredible women who showed up for me at pivotal moments. We do not do it on our own. Find your circle of mentors and sponsors and, more importantly, serve in that capacity for others when you can.

4. The practice of gratefulness is pivotal in life.

Gratitude comes from knowing I can choose my mindset and reaction to turbulence. Every day, identify the one thing you can be grateful for, and your perspective shifts to one of abundance versus one of loss. Mindset is everything.

5. Take risks, and submit to the emotional penetrability of those moments.

Open the door to new insights and ways of being in the world. It transforms you for the better. That effort enables success, tranquility, and the amplification of not just vision but lifelong abundance.

SHERLAENDER "LANI" PHILLIPS

VICE PRESIDENT, MICROSOFT, U.S. CHANNEL SALES

Sherlaender "Lani" Phillips is an award-winning, seasoned technology executive with 25 years of experience at Microsoft. Currently Vice President of U.S. Channel Sales, she leads strategy and execution supporting digital customer transformation within Microsoft's partner ecosystem. Over the years, Lani has developed a reputation for being a transformational leader committed to empowering people and driving for results.

Passionate about inspiring, transforming, and growing leaders, she hosts *Modern Mentoring with Lani Phillips,* a digital talk show designed to share wisdom globally and make mentoring accessible for all. She serves on the International Association of Microsoft Channel Partners D&I Advisory Board.

> **"Empower your team by helping them unleash their potential to achieve what they think is impossible."**

My Five Wisdoms

1. Be a game changer.

Changing the game takes courage. Get comfortable being uncomfortable, pick your battles wisely, and take on the issues that will empower your people, create new revenue streams, or make doing business with the company easier. Enlist others to collaborate to strengthen your ideas and be generous with your praise when it works. When it doesn't, fail fast, learn quickly, and pivot. Remember, failures are also successes if you learn from the experience.

2. If you don't have a plan, you become part of someone else's.

No one should put their business or career in someone else's hands. Be intentional and proactive when defining a plan, seek input from others, identify desired experiences and when you need help. Look for new ways to challenge yourself, think big, and be nimble to take advantage of unexpected opportunities.

3. Have authentic conversations.

These conversations can be difficult, especially if there's conflict involved. Have conversations in which you practice active listening and listen with empathy. Resist the urge to avoid honest conversations, and demonstrate vulnerability. Use your listening skills to deepen connections and bring resolution to conflict. As Brené Brown says, "Clear is kind." Being authentic and honest in your communication is the kind thing to do. Anything less is not kind.

4. Manage your brand.

Be intentional around defining what you want to be known for, get feedback from others to inform your progress, and be willing to adjust and evolve to stay relevant. You are an ambassador for your company and use your platform as a thought leader. Lend your voice to leverage industry events, social platforms, speaking engagements, mentoring, or blogs. Your thought leadership will strengthen your network and open doors to future success.

5. Deepen connections with your team/people.

In this modern world of work, we don't have the opportunity for as much in-person conversation as we've previously had. Find new ways to get to know your team. Prioritize having one-on-one meetings that are not just business-oriented but deeper discussions around who people are and what matters to them. Find ways to make them feel seen, valued, and heard.

CARLA GRANT PICKENS

VICE PRESIDENT, IBM GLOBAL OPERATIONS, PLATFORMS, AND DELIVERY

Carla Grant Pickens is Vice President, IBM Global Operations, Platforms, and Delivery. Carla serves on the boards for Connected DMV and Federal City Council, focusing on diversity and inclusion, education, skills, and careers in STEM in the greater DC, Maryland, and Virginia metropolitan areas. She is an executive champion for IBM's P-TECH public education model that provides high school students from underserved communities with the academic, technical, and professional skills and credentials they need for competitive STEM jobs. Carla holds a U.S. patent in retention analytics and holds the title of an IBM Inventor.

> "Use the power of your voice. It is important to 'Be Seen, Be Heard, Be Recognized' when growing your career."

My Five Wisdoms

1. Get a mentor and be a mentor.

A mentor is a role model, advisor, or counselor who can share their extensive knowledge and experiences to assist you with skills, career, or personal development. It is essential to have various mentors in your career journey. Mentor relationships should help with crucial moments of impact for your career. Most important, give back and mentor the future pipeline of diverse talent.

2. Be an ally.

Allies actively promote equality and inclusion through their committed, intentional, and positive everyday efforts to advance and benefit people different from themselves. We should use our gifts through allyship at work and in our communities with a commitment to help someone else.

3. Be seen!

It is essential to have eminence around your "expertise" and cultivate your network of colleagues. When you network, it is vital to be a social contract with people who will work with you, support, and actively engage in shared interests. Make the time to network to build relationships and expand opportunities to engage with a broader network. Share your knowledge with others.

4. Be heard.

Building skills to make you more competitive for your next role is essential. You must state your intentions of what you want and by when for your career. Having a meaningful conversation with your leader about your career aspirations is crucial.

5. Be recognized; know your worth!

Results matter. Showing accountability, action, and outcomes that matter in your efforts is important. It is equally important to have a sponsor for your career to advocate for you. Do your homework to understand the decision-makers in the room, and clearly articulate your accomplishments, impactful results, interests, and support needed for your career. Own your career, and be recognized for your work.

"Being at the top doesn't mean having all the answers—it's learning how to get those answers."

—Susan Neely

CHAPTER 4

BUSINESS ASSOCIATION INNOVATORS ADVOCATING FOR WOMEN AT WORK

These women are leading powerful, forward-thinking associations that are committed to expanding the place of women in business across the U.S. and globally. These determined women and their associations are doing amazing things. They saw an unmet need, built a mission around it, and dedicated their lives to moving women in business forward.

Each of their organizations approaches these challenges differently, yet together they reflect the energy and purpose of women working to improve society in transition. Their wisdom offers insights into what these women have experienced. Enjoy reading their ideas while embracing their commitment to change.

These business association innovators are visionaries. They are committed to changing outcomes to improve the positions, power, and pay for women. One of these leaders said: "Be comfortable with ambiguity." She knows that we cannot predict the future, but we can prepare for it, work toward it, and lend a hand to help each other along the way.

Measurable results are key indicators to capture the progress being made. Consequently, leaders of these organizations share research, resources, and best practices to enable others to sustain growth while enhancing efficiency and effectiveness. These associations are expert at broadcasting results to highlight progress as well as identify where it is lagging. Their insights and input will help you work effectively across critical areas to accelerate and achieve real results.

These associations and their innovative leaders truly understand the importance of working together for a common cause. They create new ideas, engage us, and provide a valuable platform for all of us to join.

KAREN GREENBAUM

CEO, ASSOCIATION OF EXECUTIVE SEARCH AND LEADERSHIP CONSULTANTS (AESC)

Karen Greenbaum is Chief Executive Officer of the Association of Executive Search and Leadership Consultants (AESC). AESC members are dedicated to strengthening leadership worldwide and are respected for their positive impact on the world. Karen is proud to lead a profession committed to creating a world that is inclusive, diverse, equitable, and accessible for all, helping clients develop a diverse and inclusive culture in which all feel a sense of belonging. Beginning as a secretary at Mercer and eventually becoming President and Chief Operating Officer of Mercer U.S. before joining AESC, Karen attributes her success to hard work, a positive attitude, and a willingness to take on new challenges.

> "In diversity, there is beauty and there is strength."
>
> —Maya Angelou

My Five Wisdoms

1. Attitude is the one thing you control.

One thing I learned early in my career—the importance of a positive attitude. How do people get picked for new opportunities? How do you stand out in a crowd? What makes the team, or a leader, want to work with you? A positive attitude!

2. Don't have a long-term plan.

You may miss the next great opportunity. It may seem counterintuitive, but if you stick to a plan, you may miss the next great opportunity. Don't be afraid to take risks—take on a new role, turn around a troubled business, and try something new. And don't question whether you have enough of the right experience or meet each of the requirements.

3. Network before you need to.

Think about your networks. Are you staying connected to a wide range of people? Are you building a mutually beneficial relationship and asking, "How can I help you?" whether it's an executive search consultant calling you as a source or someone from one of your networks, including your B-school alumni group, member organizations, or other? My networks include the Committee of 200, the Chicago Network, the Economic Club of Chicago, Chicago Booth, and all the members of the Association of Executive Search and Leadership Consultants, where I am CEO, as well as family and friends.

4. Be generous in helping others succeed.

Whether it's a subordinate, a peer, a friend, or someone else in your network, take pride in assisting others to succeed. One of the fastest ways to succeed is to help others and it's a great way to build a legacy authentically. Share your knowledge and experiences! Take joy in being a coach and mentor.

5. Integrity always comes first.

Your reputation is everything. It takes years to build a strong reputation based on integrity, honesty, trustworthiness, and authenticity and only an instant to destroy it. Be authentic. Always tell the truth. Practice what you preach. Don't ask others to do something you wouldn't be willing to do yourself.

NICKI KEOHOHOU

CEO, THE DIRECT SELLING WORLD ALLIANCE (DSWA) AND COACH EXCELLENCE SCHOOL

Nicki Keohohou began her career as a teacher and has been an entre-preneur most of her life. Having built successful businesses, Nicki has held executive positions, speaks at conventions globally, and consulted hundreds of companies. She's a certified business coach and emotional/ behavioral intelligence practitioner. Nicki's a bestselling author and has received numerous awards: Top 30 Female Entrepreneurs in America, Top 25 Entrepreneurs in her home state of Hawaii, and National Advocate of the Year for Working Mothers. Nicki is currently the CEO of The Direct Selling World Alliance and Coach Excellence School.

> "Self-coaching and coaching are leadership best practices. Coaching is a skill to model and replicate to empower yourself and others."

My Five Wisdoms

1. Coach yourself.

Self-coaching is a skill for self-development and performing at your best by asking yourself quality questions that challenge, inspire, and guide you to experience continued growth and progress. The quality of the questions you ask yourself are directly related to the quality of your life. Ask questions that begin with the words who, what, when, where, or how. Examples: What am I most excited about for today? Whose life will I make a difference in today? How can I reset my day?

2. Coach others.

Coaching is known for accelerating success and high performance. It gives women leaders the extra edge in their communication and supports insightful decision-making for the present and future health of the organization.

3. Add value and be of service.

The amazing thing about serving others is that it positively affects the giver. You can't give to others without also receiving benefits. Always remember that wherever you are in life, there is always someone you can make a difference for.

4. Learn from the past, live in the present, and look to the future.

Fill your life with learning experiences. The past provides you with an opportunity to learn lessons versus dwelling on your mistakes. Let go of the past that isn't serving you and appreciate the now. When you live in the present, you enjoy the magical moments in life. You have an opportunity to be present with people and situations. Research suggests that thinking about the future can help you lead a more abundant and fulfilled life. Create a life by design versus default circumstances. Design your life with a clear purpose through imagining, dreaming, journaling, visualizing, and articulating your "why."

5. Celebrate life.

Celebration creates momentum, adds fun, and is a reminder that you have made progress. Celebrations give people the time to focus on their strengths and who they are becoming while pursuing their passions. When you look for opportunities that you can celebrate in a day, you are focused on the positives and have more joy on the journey.

SUSAN NEELY

CEO, AMERICAN COUNCIL OF LIFE INSURERS (ACLI)

Susan Neely is a change-maker. Her track record of transforming industries and building consensus has revolutionized business and politics. As President and CEO of the American Council of Life Insurers, Susan forged ground-breaking initiatives to help families save for retirement, afford family leave, and tackle student loan debt. Past CEO of the American Beverage Association, she helped Pepsi and Coca-Cola navigate the sugar wars through unlikely partnerships, like Michelle Obama's Let's Move campaign. Susan was the first ever DHS Assistant Secretary for Public Affairs. She was also a two-time award winner of the CEO of the Year by her trade association and *Washingtonian*'s "100 Most Powerful Women in Washington."

> "Be the CEO of yourself. Approach every experience with purpose and determination to get the most out of it. You will always benefit."

My Five Wisdoms

1. Take calculated risks.

My dad preached the benefit of calculated risks, and he was right. Usually, the bigger the risk I've taken, the greater the success. I relied on trusted advisors who helped me measure the risk. Always be on the lookout for your support team, that "kitchen cabinet." These individuals should be champions and provocateurs who have your best interests at heart and aren't afraid to challenge your thinking.

2. Get more of what you like and less of what you don't like.

Become a lifetime learner, and be clear minded about what you like and don't like doing. Reflect occasionally: Do you like management or hate it? Are you energized by selling services or ideas? My general decision guide was to determine how to get more of what I liked and less of what I didn't like.

3. Perpetuate a cycle of lifting other voices.

Well into my career, I held a role at the Department of Homeland Security. I was once on a strategy call with top brass leaders, including Condoleezza Rice, when she was National Security Advisor. I was the newbie in the group. When I offered a point of view, another leader brushed me off. Secretary Rice jumped in, validated my point, and lifted my voice. That small action established my right to be in the group. It inspired me to do the same for others. As leaders, this costs us nothing but can be a powerful way to ensure that diverse views and ideas are heard.

4. Be comfortable with ambiguity.

As you move into your career, problems become opaquer. Learn to accept ambiguity, but know the steps to get the answers. The plan will unfold. Being at the top doesn't mean having all the answers—it's learning how to get those answers.

5. Build tough bridges.

Now more than ever, we need leaders who can keep their heads when everyone else is losing theirs. The Midwesterner in me calls this grit. But grit isn't formed by standing on your side and holding the line. Grit is developed by going through the middle, having hard conversations, and building tough bridges. Start by asking questions. You'll move from a posture of polarization to problem-solving.

LIZ SARA

PRESIDENT, SCORE FOUNDATION

———————

Liz Sara has more than 30 years of experience as a seasoned business leader, start-up champion, and entrepreneur in the national entrepreneurship community. President of the SCORE Foundation, the philanthropic arm of SCORE, the foundation supports SCORE's free small-business mentoring. She founded Best Marketing LLC, bringing C-level expertise to more than 100 early-stage companies for 20 years. Previously, she cofounded an e-commerce company, growing it to $25 million in three years. Liz has served as the presidentially appointed National Women's Business Council Chair and the first female Chair of the Dingman Center of Entrepreneurship at the University of Maryland. Liz frequently speaks at conferences and on podcasts.

> "My nod goes to baseball icon Babe Ruth, who said, 'It's hard to beat a person who never gives up.'"

My Five Wisdoms

1. We cannot ignore the men in the market because there are more of them than us.

Get used to it and figure out how to navigate to get what you want. We need men on our executive teams, on our boards, as advisors and to open doors.

2. We need to be able to talk about our business as business executives.

That means financially, too. Women must be able to speak fluently about the fundamentals of their business: cash flow, burn rate, EBITDA, etc. Too many women founders leave that to someone else. That makes them look uninformed and, worse, lacking depth.

3. Take a tip from men on how to network.

Men still get a lot of business done that way: so and so plays golf with so and so who lives next door to so and so. Suddenly, a big deal gets done because of that connection. We can do that. But we need to do it more. Don't be afraid to ask. Remember, before smartphone map apps, we were the gender that stopped the car to get directions when we got lost. Ask for help.

4. Lend a hand to other women.

Up and down the corporate ladder, women need to do a much better job at helping other women. It doesn't diminish our seat at the table when we bring another female to it. We make the table bigger. Then, when you get asked, do something to help even if you can't do everything. Just help.

5. When we make decisions, we need to act with conviction.

Men are great at this, women less so. Given the same tough decision, men will appear as if they have done it a hundred times. We need to trust ourselves and act with certainty. I've learned that very few decisions cannot be changed down the road if they do not work out. Be bold. Be confident. And act that way.

DEBORAH WINCE-SMITH

PRESIDENT AND CEO, COUNCIL ON COMPETITIVENESS

Deborah Wince-Smith is President and CEO of the Council on Competitiveness, a U.S. leadership organization of CEOs, university presidents, labor leaders, and national laboratory directors who champion national policies to improve U.S. competitiveness. She is also President of the Global Federation of Competitiveness Councils, the first global network for sharing knowledge and best practices on competitiveness. She was the first U.S. Senate-confirmed Assistant Secretary of Commerce for Technology Policy and the first Director of International Affairs in the White House Office of Science and Technology Policy, where she negotiated the landmark Head of Government Science and Technology Agreement with Japan.

> "Be a builder, not a blocker. In this era of transformation, be a positive agent of change. Create a vision that captures a future state and illuminates a path to get there."

My Five Wisdoms

1. Engage with groundbreakers, creators, and innovators—leaders who are shaping the future in our rapidly changing world.
Leaders don't stay in their comfort zones or live in stovepipes. They think outside the box, they learn, probe the perspectives of others, and seek insight from experts whose knowledge is greater than their own. Because progress depends on invention, leaders take calculated risks but recognize that some new ideas succeed and some fail.

2. Align with those who are ethical and empathetic to others.
Great leaders are ethical, believe in fair play, and walk the talk. They gain our respect, trust, and confidence by being open and honest. Leaders don't push parochial agendas; they are inclusive and care about those they seek to lead. They instill positive values and ethics in others by personally exemplifying them.

3. Reputation is the most precious thing we have.
No matter the job, strive to build a reputation of excellence, hard work, integrity, and trustworthiness. Word gets around, and it can make, break, or accelerate a career. A good reputation also adds weight to your advice, plans, and decision-making.

4. Be loyal and build loyalty.
Remember those who saw your potential, opened doors, mentored you, and helped propel your career. They invested their own reputation in you and are likely to remain a deep well of support when you need it. Nurture loyalty in others. Leaders cannot do every job, cannot make every daily decision, or see every risk on the horizon. They need people they trust to carry out critical tasks, make the right decision when it counts, and bring a problem to the table even if that might be uncomfortable.

5. Practice the Greek concept of eudaimonia—living well and doing well.
Pursue a career in which you find happiness but, in that work, can also contribute to the betterment of your field, community, or society.

"Don't miss the beauty
and joy of the positive
effect you have on people
around you."

—Theresa Harrison

CHAPTER 5

WOMEN ENTREPRENEURS CREATING BOLD, BRAVE SOLUTIONS

How do you take something you see, an idea that comes up, a new way of solving a problem, and turn it into a great, vibrant business? You become a bold and brave entrepreneur who takes a vision and turns it into a successful innovation while continuing to push the envelope to grow your businesses. These storied women are passionate performers who tell us that "failures are speed bumps on the road to success." Don't be afraid of the unknown or of taking risks. Instead, "find what you love and what brings you joy." These women might sound like "dreamers" to a non-entrepreneur, but each will change your mind and convince you to "think" big and believe in yourself. Who better than you to take an idea and make it happen?

These women have the mindset and know-how to have launched multimillion-dollar businesses. Despite obstacles, they didn't listen to anyone who said they couldn't do it. The word "no" fueled them. They are women who rise and never give up, defining the world on their terms, both in business and in their private lives. As risk-takers, movers, and shakers, they learn how to move forward a step at a time and, when needed, pick themselves up to push ahead again.

Your three authors have each started successful businesses several times. If you are ready to take your ideas and turn them into innovations, read on. These women should become your inspiration to push your businesses forward, to open new markets, and to find better solutions.

However, remember that there is a fine line between all out all the time and pausing to take care of yourself. As one of the women said, "Rest is not selfish. It is critical," as is finding your purpose in life.

SUE BURNETT

FOUNDER AND PRESIDENT, BURNETT SPECIALISTS

Sue Burnett is the Founder and President of Burnett Specialists in six Texas cities. Her 48-year-old company is the second-largest employee-owned staffing firm in the U.S., as ranked by NCEO. Sue's honors include *Houston Business Journal*'s Most Admired CEO Lifetime Achievement Award, Texas Businesswoman of the Year, WBEA Entrepreneur of the Year, and Staffing Industries' Top 100. The University of Arkansas named Sue, a distinguished alum, into the Journalism Hall of Fame. She and her husband, Rusty, were the donors for the Sue Walk Burnett Journalism and Media Center at the University of Arkansas.

> "Treat others the way they want to be treated. One of my secrets of success in my 50-year career is to treat others like your family."

My Five Wisdoms

1. Don't be afraid of taking risks.

The most significant risks of my life were primarily taken in my 20s. I moved to Houston, got a straight commission job, and started my own business at 27. When you don't take risks, you cannot win. I always felt that if it didn't work out, I could do something else.

2. Find your passion, and you will have a happy career.

I love helping people find jobs and helping women succeed in their careers. I still look forward to going to work every day after 52 years because I love the people I work with. It is exciting to have passion and purpose still! Being able to mentor other women has been so satisfying.

3. Failures are speed bumps on the road to success.

In running a company, there will be decisions that may not be successful. Failures can be learning experiences, so don't be afraid of failures. Knowing what works makes you a better businessperson.

4. Always keep learning, and be open to change.

I still go to training sessions after 50 years and take more notes than most people in the room. When you stop learning new things, you become stagnant. Also, the pandemic taught us that we can have our staff work at home and still be productive. This pandemic was a significant change for us, and I was open to it. Be flexible.

5. Being generous to others can be a great gift to yourself.

What you have in life is lost when you die, but if you give to others, it will live on after you're gone. My employee stock ownership program will provide hundreds of people with retirement money they would not have had. My building at the University of Arkansas will give students a great place to learn. Knowing that I have helped others has given me so much joy.

SHITAL DAFTARI

**FOUNDER AND CEO,
SNT BIOTECH**

Shital Daftari is a successful entrepreneur who started her business with just $3,000 from her savings and grew it into a company with over $31 million in revenue within 10 years. She is the Founder and CEO of Saris and Things and SNT Biotech and a Cofounder of Women's Empowerment Campaign, a networking and empowerment platform for South Asian women. Shital founded her company Saris and Things in 2011. In 2020, Shital pivoted her company, under the name SNT Biotech, to sell PPE, COVID-19 test kits, and lab and hospital supplies.

Shital Daftari has won many awards, including Top 50 Fastest Growing Women-Owned/Led Business by JP Morgan Chase and WPO (ranked sixth on the list in 2022), NAWBO Chicago Woman Business Owner of the Year, Enterprising Woman of the Year, Silver Stevie Award for Fastest-Growing Company of the Year, EY Entrepreneur of the Year Midwest Finalist for 2022, number 264 in the Inc. 5000 list of America's Fastest-Growing Private Companies, and the Fast 50 Asian American Business Award by USPAACC.

> "Don't be afraid to take risks. Risk and opportunity are two sides of the same coin. To achieve great success, you need to be willing to take bigger risks."

My Five Wisdoms

1. Don't be afraid to take the first step.

I firmly believe that anything is possible if you put your mind to it. All you must do is take the first step. Once you take the first step, you will see the next step and the road ahead. Don't overanalyze. Just start where you are and with what you have, and the rest will fall in place.

2. Work with the same grit and passion as the first day you started your business.

Work like your life depends on it. Don't let anyone tell you that you don't need to work hard to be successful, and don't be ashamed to work hard.

3. Find what you love. Stop doing anything that does not bring joy.

Because when you do what you love, you can put a lot of time and effort into it, and you will be able to do what it takes to be successful. If you don't love something, you will never be able to give it 100 percent.

4. Choose your fights wisely.

I have discovered that we only have limited energy for things we can fight for. I only choose to fight for the things that align with my biggest goals and dreams. Petty fights should have no place in your life.

5. Stay positive and surround yourself with people who lift you up.

For me, family is everything. Whenever I feel drained or stressed, or things are not going well, I find great strength in spending time with my family.

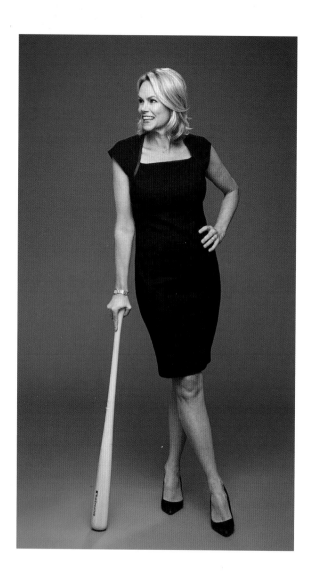

MOLLY FLETCHER

CEO, SPEAKER, AND FORMER SPORTS AGENT

Molly Fletcher is a trailblazer in every sense of the word. Hailed as "the female Jerry Maguire" by CNN, she represented sports' biggest names and negotiated over $500 million in contracts. Having been featured in ESPN, *Fast Company, Forbes,* and *Sports Illustrated,* Molly is the author of five books, most recently *The Energy Clock.* Today, Molly focuses her work on helping leaders, teams, and organizations reimagine their potential and up their game every day. A graduate of Michigan State University, Molly resides in Atlanta with her husband, Fred, and their three daughters.

> "I strive to connect, inspire, and lead with courage and optimism to bring my best self to the people and moments that matter most. The magic happens when we trade limiting beliefs for the drive to get better every day."

My Five Wisdoms

1. Develop a limitless mindset.

Where some people see obstacles, others see opportunity. Confidence can be developed one positive thought at a time and doesn't come from your comfort zone.

2. Develop a personal mission statement.

Let it serve as a compass to guide your way through the inevitable moments of discomfort and uncertainty on your way to your goals. Take time to drill down to compose your essential beliefs and personal story. It will help you understand your true self and have a motto that is easily accessible when you need it most.

3. Get clear on your purpose.

Achievement does not bring fulfillment, but purpose does. As you build connections and put your mission in motion, be relational, not transactional. You must trade self-defeating attitudes and self-imposed hurdles for a new outlook rooted in a sense of purpose. This attitude will give your life meaning.

4. Stay curious.

Curiosity and learning new things create opportunities and chances. Discovering the unknown keeps you energized. Manage your energy and selectively choose where your energy goes before the world decides for you. Even the greatest athletes in the world understand this. The playing field at work and in life requires our best effort, but staying passionate and excited helps us to go the distance.

5. Practice discipline and stay resilient.

People overestimate talent and underestimate the value and importance of discipline. Learn to be resilient by getting back up when you fall. It takes time, persistence, and keeping your eye on the ball. The difference between good and great is the ability to recover faster.

THERESA HARRISON

FOUNDER AND PRESIDENT,
GEORGE STREET SERVICES, INC.

Theresa Harrison is the Founder and President of GEORGE STREET Services, Inc., providing cloud and mobile development, cyber security solutions, project management, and managed services to government/commercial industries. Theresa solves. Theresa enjoys fitting the right pieces together to form the right team. Theresa was Cofounder and President of Athenyx, LLC, acquired in 2008. Theresa is the Founder and Partner of Kaleidoscope, which aims to increase women and minority business leaders to help launch and grow their companies. Theresa leads. Theresa is a stimulating, action-driven, sought-after speaker. Theresa shares. Theresa is the Founder of Just A Kind Note. She puts a smile on faces "one note at a time." Theresa serves.

> "Grab the hands extended to you to build your solid foundation of success and extend your hands to do the same."

My Five Wisdoms

1. Rest is not selfish. It's critical.

Stop. Pause. Step away. Resonate before resuming. Ponder. Learn how to rest. Don't miss the beauty and joy of the positive effect you have on people around you. Listen to what your body, mind, and heart are saying. Don't devalue rest. Do not continually push through. We have attached value to how busy we are. How much we have on our plates, how many invitations we have, how many businesses we started. These things don't tell you how you're doing. They tell you what you're doing. Build in rest time and get ready for more celebrations.

2. Celebrate you!

Celebrate and enjoy your journey. The road traveled in leadership is bumpy, long, tough, stressful, challenging, and lonely. Choose to celebrate all milestones, big and small. Celebrate wins and successes. Leadership is challenging, so why not reward yourself? Celebrations build up your confidence to keep moving forward. This is your call forward. This is your time. This is the moment you have worked for, looked for, and dreamed of for so long. Celebrate what you have accomplished today, and then keep moving forward.

3. Perfection is not the goal.

You don't have to be perfect. Don't wait to reach perfection, or you will be waiting a lifetime. There is no perfect time, day, customer, or solution. Allow yourself the opportunity to improve, develop, and grow.

4. Share your story of success.

Believe in your accomplishments. Be confident. Show your courage. Let others see you. Stop shrinking. Acknowledge your achievements. Stand up. Shine. Show your impact.

5. Empower your team.

Don't try to do everything. Empower your team, who are complimentary, committed, and vested in your vision and culture. Support your team's proven ability to be good at what they do. Overinvest in the team. Hire the best people. Attract, motivate, and reward your team. Give trust. Give independence. Give praise. Give freedom. Encourage. Your team will give back more than they were given.

FELICITY HASSAN

FOUNDER, THEFIND

Felicity Hassan is a published author and Founder of TheFind, a search firm committed to finding great talent between the lines. Raised by hardworking parents and committed to earned rewards, she worked full-time for Red Bull as a student. On graduation, she joined Michael Page, building teams in London and New York, and was tapped to join Leathwaite, a search boutique firm. In this role, she was approached by her client, Bloomberg, to build a global talent platform. Felicity followed their CPO to Audible and spent another few years before returning to the search world to pursue her passion for building representative leadership.

> "Know your numbers! Data is critical to every business decision. You can have the numbers without the story, but never the story without the numbers."

My Five Wisdoms

1. Be authentic.
Think through your company's strategic objectives and core values, tap into where these intersect with your superpowers, and don't hold back.

2. Leverage allies.
Straight white men still dominate business leadership. We know that employees who have influential sponsors will tend to go further faster. Finding an ally who can sponsor you through your organization is of equal if not more excellent value than endeavoring to seek out a leader that looks like you. These folks are fewer in number and in greater demand, so their ability to offer you the support you need may be limited.

3. Find support.
The most excellent advice I was given early in my career was by a senior female executive, wife, and mother. She shared that no one would applaud me for doing it all; they would come to expect it. Identify the tasks in life and work you can effectively delegate to buy yourself time to be more productive or present. Invest in outsourcing.

4. Be curious.
If change is the constant, then embrace it. Different generations think differently. Technology is hard to keep up with as it rapidly evolves. Process change can be both exciting and disruptive. Having the confidence to approach change with curiosity, positivity, and an open mind will set you apart from your peers.

5. Stop working so hard.
In my career, I have often had that nagging feeling that I was playing catch up. If you entertain this voice, you should expect to hit burnout. Take some tips from your male counterparts; make a concerted effort to secure projects that play to your strengths, but don't feel the need to outwork your peers. You will overstretch and under-deliver. Find your metaphorical "golf course" and build fun in your work and life. It's incredible what can be achieved when you hit pause, lift your head, and take a good look around.

ASMA ISHAQ

CEO, MODERE

Asma Ishaq is the CEO of Modere, a pioneer of the collagen industry and a thought leader in the natural health and wellness space. NutraIngredients awarded Asma NutraChampion in 2020, the same year she was named Chair of the Collagen Stewardship Alliance. In 2021, she earned recognition as a *Forbes* Top 10 CEO and catapulted Modere to number one on the 50 Fastest Growing Women-Led Companies list, where she has ranked among the top five from 2019 to 2022. She is a winner of Ernst & Young's illustrious EY Entrepreneur of the Year 2022 Pacific Southwest Award.

> "Never let anyone else dictate your destiny."

My Five Wisdoms

1. Know your worth and speak your truth.
In my experience, many women are reluctant to ask for what they believe they deserve. Not standing up for yourself is a deficiency you can and should overcome. To counter that reluctance, I actively encourage the women in my company to share ideas and opinions, make it a point to praise their work when appropriate, make sure they are paid commensurately, and always keep the lines of communication open.

2. Collaborate.
Your peers are an invaluable source of support and inspiration. I have had the privilege of getting to know an array of highly talented women business leaders through peer leadership groups such as the Women Business Collaborative (WBC), the Committee of 200 (C200), the Women Presidents Organization (WPO), and the Young Presidents Organization (YPO). In committing to support one another and freely sharing ideas and experiences, we continue to inspire and encourage one another to greater and greater heights.

3. Pay it forward and mentor.
To reach gender parity and seat more women at the table, we must apply the same generosity of spirit to support and inspire up-and-coming women leaders. Research indicates that mentorship is highly effective for women and ethnic minorities. I take great pride in being a mentor to several young women at various stages of their careers. And I continue to meet with my mentor, who pushes me to keep aspiring to the next level.

4. Continue to educate yourself personally and professionally.
I read a lot, especially books on leadership. I also regularly read trusted business journals to keep abreast of the latest strategies and trends in business today.

5. Be resourceful.
When you reach an impasse, find another route. Be bold and enterprising. Know when and where to look for help and how to ask.

MARGERY KRAUS

FOUNDER AND EXECUTIVE CHAIRMAN, APCO WORLDWIDE

Margery Kraus is the Founder and Executive Chairman of APCO Worldwide, a global advisory and advocacy communications consultancy headquartered in Washington, DC, and the world's largest women-owned communications firm. Margery has deep expertise in providing strategic counsel on issue-based communication, crisis management, market-entry, and corporate reputation across diverse industry groups. Margery is active on many institutional and corporate boards and committees in the industry. She is Chair of the Women Presidents Organization, is on the international advisory board of Tikehau Capital, and is a Trustee of American University and many others.

> "The saying 'where there's a will, there's a way' has been around for a long time. Such an old phrase is still relevant."

My Five Wisdoms

1. Never underestimate the value of being underestimated.

I learned that if people are prejudiced or biased, use it to your advantage because they will never see you coming. I can provide scores of examples of how I was able to come away with deals done and challenges accomplished just because I was able to out-maneuver those who underestimated me. If people are blind to confidence and success, I use it in a way that is helpful to what I want to achieve.

2. Be more prepared to be heard.

Unfortunately, women still must do this. I can ask women in business this question, and I know the answer: How many times have you said something really smart, and no one listens, and then a man says the same thing, and the consensus in the room is it's the best idea they have ever heard? Come to every meeting fully prepared and ensure your ideas are heard by speaking up.

3. The ultimate reward in life and a career well spent must come from inside you.

You must drive your own personal self-satisfaction. To be a happy and fulfilled person, you must learn to reach inside and find that satisfaction within you; it doesn't come from others. If you wait for that to come, you may be very disappointed in life.

4. Create your network of colleagues and friends.

I have certain friends who give me joy just by being near them. Other friends are experts in their fields and can offer advice and test my judgment. Other friends don't take anything; they just give. I've found that the more you give, the more you get. This mosaic of fantastic relationships helps shape my life. Create your mosaic of friendships and relationships that enrich your life, both personally and professionally.

5. "No one can make you feel inferior without your own consent." (Eleanor Roosevelt)

When you have those self-doubts, the most important thing is to believe in yourself and not worry about how others make you feel.

SHARON W. REYNOLDS

ENTREPRENEUR AND CEO, DEVMAR PRODUCTS, LLC, AND DEVMAR MANUFACTURING
A MULTI-AWARD-WINNING SERIAL ENTREPRENEUR

Sharon W. Reynolds, President and CEO of DevMar Products, LLC, began her company in 2007 to develop and distribute environmentally friendly products that eradicate pathogens while creating healthy spaces and sustaining the environment. By 2011, DevMar was recognized as a "Green Hero" of Nashville by the *Nashville Post* and Nashville Area Chamber of Commerce. In 2012, DevMar received the Women Impacting Public Policy Business Leadership External Communications award. Sharon was honored among the 2021 Women to Watch by the *Nashville Medical News*. Enterprising Women selected Sharon as one of the Top 20 in 2020 Award Recipients among 1,000 top women entrepreneurs, and in 2022, Sharon received recognition as an Academy of Women Achievers, the highest honor for women bestowed by the YWCA.

> "Gender equity is a fundamental human right and a core foundation for a peaceful, prosperous, and sustainable world. Use your talent to transform the next generation."

My Five Wisdoms

1. Lead by example.

Empowerment lies in collaboration. Promoting parity and equity for all women is a personal vision and mission. Join me as I participate in high-profile organizations such as the Women Business Collaborative and the International Women's Forum, where I lend my voice to support and promote women. When a seasoned businesswoman takes the bold step to help another woman grow her business, we recognize the beautiful dynamics in our mutual-support communities.

2. Share your pitfalls and victories.

The pitfalls of an entrepreneur can be vast. Focusing on where you are going and "growing" is paramount for me. So, what have I learned? A clear focus on a destination with clarity is essential. Take the time to carve out those steps. It will save you from a lot of frustration.

3. Access is the order of the day. What does that mean?

Women continue to trail behind men in gaining access to capital. The statistics are crippling and create a significant void in women's business progression. Women, especially women of color, not only earn less than men in the workforce but are also less likely to gain access to capital for their businesses. It is time for equal pay, parity, and power.

4. Giving back. You can't take it with you!

Giving back encompasses so many ways we can make an impact in our communities and positively affect the lives each of us touches. There are many ways to give back:

- Serving on boards where decisions are made to change lives.
- Giving our means.
- Mentoring to help women grow.

5. Think and work with your community. It will thank you.

Remember that your impact is far broader than your wonderful family, business, and others you touch. There is a world that needs your support. How you share with others and care about them becomes part of who you are as a trailblazing woman.

ILENE G. ROSENTHAL

CEO AND FOUNDER, FOOTSTEPS2BRILLIANCE

Ilene G. Rosenthal is the CEO and Founder of Footsteps2Brilliance, a break-through bilingual educational software company that accelerates student achievement by uniting the power of mobile gaming with the latest in cognitive research. Footsteps2Brilliance has won numerous awards, including SIIA Codie Finalist for "Best K-12 Instructional Solution," AEP prize for "Best ESL/ELL Solution," and Gold Winner for the National Parenting Publications Awards. It has been recognized by the White House Initiative on Educational Excellence for Hispanics and the Clinton Global Initiative and has been honored by the United Nations, World Bank, and UNICEF for its work helping to democratize education for children throughout the world.

> "Think BIG! I was inspired by my grandfather, who loved to quote Daniel Burnham: 'Make no little plans. They have no magic to stir men's blood and probably will not themselves be realized . . .'"

My Five Wisdoms

1. Begin with an incredible team.

Hire the right talent, mentor and develop them, and you will thrive. Teams come in different styles and sizes. Make sure you know the type of team you need to perform at the highest levels for your business. Watch to see how the team players adapt to change, because you will grow, and so will they.

2. Choose the right partner.

You will inevitably go through twists and turns as you develop your successful innovations. Partners complement your viewpoint and skillset, bringing different experiences and perspectives to help you develop great business solutions. Shared ideas generate new ways of doing things, far better than any one person can do on their own.

3. Success is grounded in the culture.

My staff repeatedly told us that they love the way we work together. We live our values and enable them to do the same. If you don't intentionally create your organization's culture, people will create one for you, and it may not be the one that you want or that works well.

4. Passion is essential, as is a clear purpose.

Think about it. You are going to have roadblocks, detours, and challenges. Without the power of your passion supported by your purpose, you will easily find yourself moving in the wrong direction. Passion will help you stay focused over the long term, and your purposeful drive will sustain your momentum.

5. Technology is your friend.

Technological options open new ways to innovate. Find those that enable you to grow your business by engaging with your customers. Technology should make it easy, simple, and fun to work with your company and your team.

JOYCE SALZBERG

CEO, SUNNY DAYS

A recognized leader and innovator in early intervention, Joyce Salzberg has over 40 years of experience in health care and developmental disabilities. She serves on New Jersey's State Interagency Coordinating Council and is currently the Chair. Joyce cofounded Sunny Days in 1994, one of the nation's leading early intervention and autism services providers, serving children throughout the United States, China, and Latin America. Prior, she held various positions in the field of developmental disabilities. Having also served on charitable boards, oversight committees, and advocacy groups, she believes in giving back to others. Joyce holds a BA and MSW from Temple University, where she's on the board and has been honored and inducted into the Gallery of Success (2013).

> "The word 'persistence' defines how I got through many tough times. As Churchill stated, 'Never, never, never give up.' That's my mantra as well."

My Five Wisdoms

1. Embrace change.

One principle of social work is to effect change. It's an easy concept to explain but not easy to follow. As an entrepreneur, I worked with teams to raise our businesses from the ashes of the pandemic. Our model had to change in a single day. These changes brought the increased acceptance of telehealth and remote/hybrid work models, allowing us to better support the families we serve.

2. Express gratitude by paying it forward.

As a woman from a humble background, I'm often surprised at how my success transpired when I look back at what I've accomplished. Years ago, when an all-male Board of Trustees fired me from United Cerebral Palsy of New Jersey for having had breast cancer, I was supported by other women who knew me and my skills. This experience ultimately led to the company I run today, Sunny Days Early Childhood Developmental Services.

3. Acknowledge your successes, and support others in their efforts.

My generous gift to fund the Center for Professional Development at Temple University's College of Liberal Arts came from this mindset. I hope to inspire students and alums who aspire to academic and professional success.

4. Lift other women.

Be the conduit to support other women in expressing their thoughts and increasing their success. When women's rights are still being abrogated, we must support one another.

5. Network, network, network.

I frequently meet with students at Temple University and have been on panels with the College of Liberal Arts. I often discuss the importance of networking. Cultivating relationships is one of the essential stepping-stones to success. Even in brief encounters, one can tell the proverbial "elevator story." You never know how that might affect them or who they may know to assist in your endeavors.

GEMMA TONER

FOUNDER AND CEO, TONE NETWORKS

Gemma Toner is a media and telecommunications leader known for driving innovation. In 2017, Gemma created Tone Networks, a SAAS micro-learning platform designed for early to mid-career women to stay and advance in the workplace. She's been a board member of publicly traded companies, including Sandvine and Engagement Labs, Chairperson for CTAM, and board member of multiple women's organizations. Before founding Tone, Gemma held executive positions in media and technology for AMC and Cablevision Media, running the fastest ISP in the country. Additionally, she has been granted patents for data analytics. Gemma proudly serves the global humanitarian organization Concern Worldwide.

> "Find the courage to ask why not; if not me, then who? If not now, then when? Be brave, and make the move that scares you. That's where you'll discover your greatness!"

My Five Wisdoms

1. Just start.

"Just start and then keep going" is truly the best advice I ever received from one of my mentors. There are plenty of times when we are not quite sure how to begin or feel that what we are working on is not ready or good enough. Here is the thing. Start anyway, because by starting, you learn, you see what works, and while you might make lots of mistakes, you adjust and nail it.

2. Jump around. Be open to lateral moves.

There are many ways to build your career. Mine was a bit of trial and error. I could identify what I didn't like, but it took me longer to figure out what I liked and enjoyed. When I took on roles I was not wild about, I enjoyed them the most. This led to bigger opportunities. Sometimes you don't know what you don't know. Be open and curious.

3. Raise your hand early and often.

You might not get the job or be picked for the project, but some of the biggest opportunities I have had in my career were by default. I was not the first choice. When you get the right chance, you'll be better prepared to run with it.

4. Remember where you came from.

My immigrant father built a successful business and shared this with me all the time. Each one of us has had some help along the way. Success is a team sport. We all need someone who believes in us more than we do ourselves. Share your wisdom and experiences with other women.

5. Practice grace.

We all have had setbacks and are going to have more setbacks. You can let them define you and limit you, or you can find the grace to handle the disappointment and learn as much as you can from it. Then, let it go and move on.

"Purpose: My most successful projects have been those with a mission to make an impact."

—DeLisa Guerrier

CHAPTER 6

WOMEN BUSINESS CREATORS AND INNOVATORS TRANSFORMING IDEAS INTO ACTION

Each woman in this chapter is uniquely gifted with energy, creativity, and personal strength, and the breadth of their ingenuity will fascinate you. Some of the women are world leaders in clothing design. Another has had a lifelong passion for finding better, quality-based cosmetics for women. One has a very rare, vertically integrated fashion brand.

Think about your own inner creative genius. It is there, perhaps in hiding, but you might be sitting on the next big idea. When a "big" idea comes to you, do you dismiss it, dwell on it, or take it to heart? Learn from these women who are driven by bringing their ideas to life.

What do their stories tell you? Believe that you have what it takes to create and succeed, especially if the idea is original. As you think about your ideas, declare yourself early and often. It is time for you to discover what is right before you.

Women business creators and innovators are leaving their unique imprint and mark. We admire their stick-to-it-ness and are inspired by their determination. These women are doers, capturing great ideas that can make a difference. As knowledge seekers, they embrace lifetime learning.

As women who have grown with others, they look to see how to help women in their careers. They care deeply about giving back.

You'll notice a recurring theme. While they are very successful, these women never sound like they have arrived. Instead, they are driven by pushing forward to make things better. Always curious, testing, and trying, they see what is possible and want to achieve it.

Welcome these women whose companies have prospered as they pushed beyond what is today so they can create tomorrow.

TACY M. BYHAM, PhD

CEO, DDI

Tacy M. Byham, PhD, is the Chief Executive Officer of DDI. DDI works side by side with executives to find and grow ready-now and ready-next leaders who can make powerful leadership decisions and navigate global complexity. They help organizations confidently build a framework for success through the science and practice of leadership strategy, selection, development, and succession management.

Tacy and the consultants at DDI interact with boards of directors regularly, completing 70 global CEO assessments annually for Fortune 500s, family-owned businesses, and nonprofits. DDI's world-class learning systems help our client organizations develop more than 250,000 better leaders for a better future every year.

> **"#LeadLikeAGirl: To be successful, happy, and fulfilled in work/life, it's less about acting more like a man or more like a woman. It is about becoming the best-ever version of yourself."**

My Five Wisdoms

1. Power move: find your strength and the leader within you.

Eleanor Roosevelt said, "A woman is like a tea bag. You never know how strong she is until she gets in hot water." Thus, we need to educate women and their allies on the following "Power Moves" to amplify women in the workplace and ignite change.

2. Power move: declare yourself early and often.

Telling yourself to declare your readiness for the next step up is no more than a personal aspirational goal. Consider your allies/coaches/HR business partners like DDI who can inspire you to change your approach to leadership for yourself, the women you mentor and lead, and the daughters you are raising from this generation of the workforce and in the future.

3. Power move: explore the confidence gap.

Research clearly shows no real difference between genders regarding leadership ability. Is it a matter of confidence? DDI's own Global Leadership Forecast research echoes this theme, with women tending to evaluate themselves as less effective leaders than their male peers. While everyone needs confidence, women sometimes need a different voice in their head, helping them to declare themselves and be bold. Words matter! There is language you can use to maximize and project confidence. (And other phrases you may find yourself saying inadvertently undermine the confidence you project to others.) Seek expert advice as you project a more confident voice. These tips are essential to be a leader.

4. Power move: identify your personal wake-up call.

What we don't know about how business works also holds us back. And we can do something about that every day. Your leadership allies can help you find your story.

5. Power move: superpower your network.

Now more than ever, you need to create a small networking and support group that helps you grow yourselves as professionals and helps you navigate what will make you successful at your company. It absolutely IS who you know that will make a difference in your career!

TENA CLARK

CEO AND FOUNDER, DMI MUSIC & MEDIA SOLUTIONS

Tena Clark, CEO and Chief Creative Officer for DMI Music & Media Solu-
tions, is one of the most influential female producers in the music industry and
American media. From her early years, discovered by Stevie Wonder, to her
multiple Grammy awards, she has written for and produced award-winning
legends such as Aretha Franklin, Natalie Cole, Patti Labelle, Dionne Warwick,
LeAnn Rimes, Chaka Khan, and Maya Angelou. She was commissioned to
write theme songs for NASA and Hillary Clinton, and her work spans film,
television, stage, records, and brands. A civil rights activist and a crusader for
women and the LGBTQ community, she is the author of the memoir *South-
ern Discomfort*.

> "Love is the one thing that defines success. I define success by loving what I do, so much so that it does not feel like work. The other is having a meaningful family life. Women do not need to pick between a career or family."

My Five Wisdoms

1. Ask yourself, what can you do?

I ask myself that question often. I can stand with my brothers and sisters. I can vote. I can keep up the fight. I can show up. I can use my voice. I can be an example and teach my children and their children that we are more alike than different and that we are all equal.

2. Permit other women to dream.

I grew up in rural Mississippi and am dedicated to helping underprivileged women in the South. I believe the underserved and disadvantaged women will change this world. Whether it's encouragement or financing, it takes so little to make a difference in someone's life who doesn't know they can dream. I want them to be mentored and realize they can make a difference.

3. March to the beat of a different drum.

I wanted to play the drums, and my parents said I could not play the drums because the drums were not for girls. That's like waving a red flag in front of a bull. I bet with my older sister when I was 10 since all I thought about was music and said: "By the time I'm 35, I'm going to be somebody."

4. Become a natural saleswoman.

In a 2012 *Forbes* interview, I said I could "sell fire to the devil." Whether it was pitching songs or music strategy, I had to believe in it 150 percent to sell it. If you don't believe in what you're selling, get out, because BS is not for sale.

5. Tell your story.

I am a storyteller, whether that story comes out in a song, a book, a TV show, a film, or on stage. Storytelling changes people's hearts and minds. Share your story about how you want to be remembered. I want to be remembered for my compassion, my music, and being a loving spouse, mother, and grandmother.

DeLISA GUERRIER

**MANAGING PARTNER, GUERRIER DEVELOPMENT;
CEO AND FOUNDER, STORYVILLE GARDENS**

DeLisa Guerrier is an accomplished real estate executive and entrepreneur and is one of the few Black women in the state of Tennessee licensed as a general contractor for commercial, residential, and industrial development. She guides Guerrier Development's vision for communities and drives its social mission to invest in emerging neighborhoods. DeLisa is well known for her business acumen, but her latest project is receiving international attention. Born from the desire to inspire literacy and unlock a child's imagination, DeLisa created Storyville Gardens, an innovative and interactive theme park based on stories from the four corners of the world.

> "Before taking my nine-hour contractor exam, my mother said, 'Everything you need to take this step, you already possess.' I repeat this mantra with every step forward in my life. I have what it takes!"

My Five Wisdoms

1. Prepare to sacrifice.

Most journeys of significance require a path less traveled and a path that does not look pretty to receive the greatest reward later down the road. Get prepared. It will pay back in droves when choosing to invest in your goals instead of taking a vacation, buying that designer handbag, or hanging out with friends.

2. The law of increasing return.

Most of the time, when a journey begins, we're not where we want to be. I challenge people to put 150 percent into whatever they are doing, even if it's not where their heart is. You never know when opportunities and resources will show up to further a goal; it could easily pop up when an individual feels like they're stuck in a dead-end job. Imagine the opportunities that will pass you by if you don't show up every day ready to give it your all.

3. One step, every day.

I get overwhelmed looking at the entire forest instead of focusing on the tree directly in front of me. I encourage people to take one step toward their goal every day; when they look back over time, they will see how far they've come.

4. Three things to focus on:

• People: Put the right team together because it takes a team to execute.

• Package: Put a package together so people can see the vision.

• Purpose: My most successful projects have been those with a mission to make an impact. Connecting to a purpose bigger than the return comes with a level of fulfillment that money doesn't buy.

5. Seek humility.

I believe in the strength of humility and am always ready to learn. Every situation has a lesson to it. However, if we are too prideful, we will miss it.

LILI HALL

CEO AND PRESIDENT, KNOCK, INC.

Lili Hall is the Founder and CEO of KNOCK, Inc., a Minneapolis-based independent creative agency leading strategic brand development and design thinking on a national and international scale. She's a visionary and an entrepreneur at heart with an unwavering commitment to greater inclusion for women and BIPOC populations—manifested through partnerships on boards, DEI initiatives, and networks, including the Global Thinkers Forum. Named one of EY's Entrepreneurial Winning Women and Most Admired CEO by *Minneapolis-St. Paul Business Journal,* Lili measures success on her company's culture, growth, and profitability and through her far-reaching impact on businesses, brands, and communities.

> "The collective wisdom we share as women is exponential. When we collaborate freely, we know we can make the greatest impact in business—in life."

My Five Wisdoms

1. Be wise.

Wisdom is foundational to business success. I've often sought the knowledge of women who've come before me. The greatest for me was my mother, who taught me that I could be anything I put my heart and mind to. Her sage advice has shaped me as a business leader. It's now incumbent upon me to extend those learnings to a new generation of women. Sharing wisdom is our mandate. It can be done individually as a mentor or collectively through supportive networks, organizations, and initiatives.

2. Be kind.

As a Brazilian American woman, I learned to be respectful of people from other cultures, backgrounds, identities, and abilities. My global perspective is synonymous with the golden rule of treating others as you would want to be treated. When I see civil unrest and injustices, I support those historically excluded from the conversation. Empathy and selflessness are required for effective leadership.

3. Be curious.

We are all more exciting and thought-provoking if we bring fresh, new ideas to the table. Pushing yourself to think beyond the construct of everyday business practices will elevate your leadership practice and give you differentiating value. One way to do that is to ask questions continually. Listening to other people's opinions can help shape your own. We have much to experience from each other.

4. Be collaborative.

Being collaborative is the hallmark of my life. We can do so much more together than either of us on our own. Since the pandemic, I've learned that collaboration is achieved just as much in a physical room as on a digital screen. One underlying theme that fosters good collaboration is trust. Learning to trust each other will break down the boundaries that stifle us and allow for the free exchange of ideation.

5. Be exceptional.

The previous four actionable values add up to being an exceptional human being. It is the grand crescendo to being the best possible woman business leader. Let's all be good advocates for each other.

KATE ISLER

CEO, THEWMARKETPLACE

Kate Isler is the CEO of TheWMarketplace, the economic engine for women, and Cofounder of Be Bold Now, a nonprofit focused on accelerating gender parity. With over 20 years of international executive leadership experience working for Fortune 100 companies, Kate's journey of leadership, overcoming adversity, and breaking gender stereotypes motivates and inspires. Her experiences as CEO of a digital health start-up and as an executive at Microsoft provide powerful real-world examples when addressing gender equity and balanced management practices. Kate shares her insights in her memoir, *Breaking Borders* (2021), and as contributing writer for *Entrepreneur Magazine, Thrive,* and *Glass Hammer.*

> "Women supporting women will change the world! My mission is to create opportunities for women to support one another and live to our fullest potential."

My Five Wisdoms

1. Follow your passion, no matter how unattainable it feels.

Many of us self-select out of following our passion. We believe we must have all the items on some imaginary list to achieve this passion. Tear up this list!! I encourage women to replace the doubt that comes with trying to fit the checklist with "Why not me?" and start envisioning themselves living their passion.

2. Commit to act.

Action is important, even if you discover that you need to adjust your direction or even move backward a few steps. Waiting until the time is "right" to act inevitably turns into nonaction. The time will NEVER be perfect. Take a step forward and then assess the situation with each step and make it the right time by adapting to the situation.

3. Tell your story.

When women share stories, two things happen: (1) We immediately find common ground because of similar experiences or connect with a shared emotion. (2) We inspire one another to take bold action. We see ourselves in each other and realize, "If she can do that, I can do it too!" Inspire one another. Tell your story. You won't be disappointed and may change another woman's life.

4. Create a "council."

I am fortunate to have a group of BOLD women around me who have generously shared their feedback, insights, love, and advice throughout my career. These are people who raise their voices and celebrate with me and the ones who will tell me the hard truths when needed and that I may not want to hear. My council enriches my life every day, and it has been crucial for my professional and personal life. Everyone needs a council.

5. Join TheWMarketplace!

TheWMarketplace is my tool to change the world and create economic gender equality. Money is power. Buying from and supporting women-owned businesses will have a direct positive impact on their economic platform. Everyone can shop on TheWMarketplace and support hundreds of women-led companies in a very tangible way. If you are a woman-owned business, join us as a sales channel for your merchandise or service.

KIMBER MADERAZZO

BEAUTY LEADER AND ACTIVIST

Kimber Maderazzo is a seasoned executive and experienced board member. She has led entrepreneurial companies and been an operating advisor in private equity firms. At the helm of critical initiatives, she has successfully propelled innovative growth strategies and radical change within the beauty, cosmetics, and health industries for over 25 years. In her most recent role, she led the integration of the world's largest acne-fighting brand, Proactiv, into a joint venture with Nestlé Switzerland. She also serves as Chairman of the Board for C200; on the Advisory Board for Musely, a leader in telemedicine skin; and as Director at Large at Synergy Life Science, a technology company.

> "Women have the power to change the world. As leaders, we must encourage and help facilitate these networking relationships that build women's confidence and competence."

My Five Wisdoms

1. Be intentional.

Create strong relationships with people who will be able to influence your growth. I've witnessed the power of a peer community collaborating with like-minded women, building their companies with the help of robust support systems. I've seen the starring role in the success that networks play as they provide access to ideas, resources, support, and mentorship.

2. Collaborate.

Find areas where opportunities with others will push you faster and farther. I learned early on to push myself and to be intentional about building my networks. I'm passionate about helping other women to do the same. I'm a proponent of a broad network that can help open doors and a deep personal network to discuss complex topics and serve as a private board of advisors.

3. Lose the hook.

Unhook yourself from unhealthy competitiveness. Negativity will always pull you in the wrong direction if you do not.

4. Create impressions.

Always remember that how you act contributes to how others will remember you. There are many ways to create beauty in life. Your actions offer an inside view into who you are and what you stand for.

5. Stay connected.

Don't forget that others move on to bigger and better opportunities. You want them to think of you when something comes up. Knowing how to network strategically is a potent business tool necessary at all career stages. The secret to success is being intentional about how you connect with others. Essential business relationships must be sought out and nurtured.

DEIRDRE QUINN

COFOUNDER AND CEO, LAFAYETTE 148 NEW YORK

Deirdre Quinn is the Cofounder and CEO of Lafayette 148 New York, one of the few genuinely vertically integrated fashion houses worldwide. Before founding L148 in 1996 with two other fashion veterans and visionaries, Shun Yen Siu and Ida Siu, Deirdre worked as the Vice President of Production at Liz Claiborne, Donna Karan, and Escada. She was awarded the Ernst & Young Entrepreneur of the Year 2016 Award. In 2018, Deirdre was recognized with the Corporate Leadership Award from Fashion Group International and an Elly Award, honoring outstanding women leaders of the Women's Forum of New York. Deirdre has a lifelong love of learning and devotion to philanthropy and is inspired to enrich the world through education. She currently serves as a member of the Fashion Institute of Technology's Board of Trustees.

> "Keep building. As an entrepreneur and the leader of a women-led business, we're setting the stage for the future to be at the forefront of change and evolution."

My Five Wisdoms

1. Build a strong team.
Create a company culture that reflects your core values with innovative, like-minded people. Keep learning.

2. Focus. Find your passion.
Learn patience and persistence, then learn to be faster and better. Know who you are (or who you are not).

3. Problem solve.
Never stop changing. Work smarter. Be open-minded to change and evolve. When you find a problem, fix it fast.

4. Take calculated risks.
Don't spend what you don't have. It's hard to make money and easy to spend.

5. Be patient and don't compromise.
The quality of your output is nonnegotiable. Stay true to your brand.

JUDI SHEPPARD MISSETT

FOUNDER AND EXECUTIVE CHAIR, JAZZERCISE, INC.

Judi Sheppard Missett is the Founder and Executive Chair of Jazzercise, Inc., the world's largest and longest-lasting franchise dance fitness company. From a single class in 1969, Judi has piloted Jazzercise through five decades of continuous growth to today's 8,000 franchisees teaching 32,000 classes a week worldwide, generating $78 million in annual revenue. She is a renowned fitness expert and exercise pioneer and has received numerous prestigious awards. These include the Presidential Commendation for Top Women Entrepreneurs, four Hall of Fame inductions, and the Sports Entrepreneur of the Year Award. Judi's national bestselling book *Building a Business with a Beat* was deemed "indispensable for entrepreneurs."

> "Follow your passion. It will fuel you to work really hard, attract others to your mission, and persist until you achieve communal success."

My Five Wisdoms

1. Change is inevitable; embrace it.

Once you accept that life and your business are an ongoing process of creation and re-creation, you can strive for a constant innovation cycle. At Jazzercise, people marvel that we've racked up five decades of continuous growth in the fad-driven physical fitness industry. How? By listening to our customers, embracing their need for change and challenge, updating our product line every 10 weeks, and reinventing our business model every 10 years.

2. Learn to negotiate.

Most people see negotiation as a game of winner versus loser. At Jazzercise, we negotiate everything—leases, contracts, schedules—with the goal of a mutually beneficial win-win. We work hard to identify the other person's needs, understand the hard yes, the flexible no, and lean heavily on the magical power of "What if?" and "Why not?" Also, please don't make the mistake of thinking negotiating is all about money; frequently, it's not.

3. Create winning situations all around for everyone.

Beyond negotiating, examine every aspect of your business—products, services, profitability—through the lens of "How can I create a winning situation for my customers, my employees, and my company?" If it's not a win-win-win, we won't do it.

4. Hone your decision-making.

Being the decision-maker can be tough, especially when it involves major course-correcting choices. My personal process is "head, heart, and gut." First, mentally analyze the situation to determine what you think about your options. Next, sit with each option to discover how you feel about it. Finally, check in with your gut; that inner voice encompasses all your passion, experience, strength, talents, skills, mishaps, and learned lessons. When your head, heart, and gut agree, proceed. If not, pause to listen to your hesitation. That still, small inner voice will never steer you wrong.

5. Make the body-mind-spirit connection.

You are so much more than your thoughts and feelings. While your mind may predominate, your body is the wellspring of strength, resilience, and longevity. And your spirit is the source of joy and peace. Think you don't have time to exercise or explore your spirituality? The truth is . . . time is all any of us have. Connecting to your body, mind, and spirit will help you make the most of it in business and life.

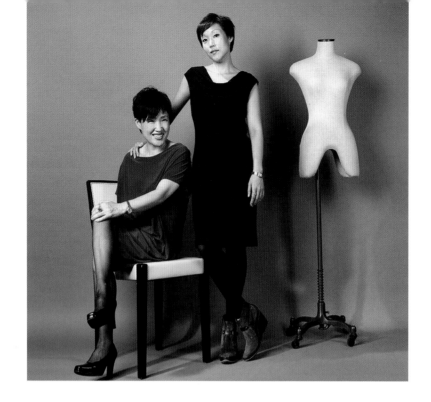

CLARA SUNWOO
DESIGNER AND FOUNDER, CLARA SUNWOO

ROSEANN SUNWOO
CEO AND FOUNDER, CLARA SUNWOO

Clara and Roseann Sunwoo are the NYC mother-daughter Founders of Clara Sunwoo, an ageless women's lifestyle brand known for timeless style, comfort, and a perfect fit with a modern edge. Clara immigrated from Seoul, Korea, to NYC in 1975 with a suitcase and $1,000. The Clara Sunwoo collection was born out of hands-on artistry. In 1997, she began the brand with her daughter Roseann, whose entrepreneurial spirit as CEO innovated the signature, award-winning fabric "liquid leather." Clara Sunwoo has grown into a national success with independent boutiques in all 50 states and a solid direct-to-consumer presence.

> "The modern woman is ageless and fearless, and the fashion industry must not categorize her. We are obsessed with changing the way women think about style and comfort. Our mantra: 'Make women FEEL good and spread joy one woman at a time.'"

My Five Wisdoms

1. Ask for help, know when to reach out, and don't be afraid to ask.

It took us decades to understand you can accelerate years of knowledge in one meeting. We tend to be "doers." Remind yourself of the importance of asking for help.

2. Relationships are key.

Our early relationships led to some of our best partnerships today. For over 25 years, we have worked with many of the same mills, vendors, and clients, building mutual trust and respect. Our most meaningful relationships were made over time and come from seeds that developed deep roots. Too often, we see people handing out business cards and working a room to meet as many contacts as possible. Think quality over quantity.

3. Follow through on your commitments, and make your word impeccable.

If you commit, commit 100 percent. Always present your best work, and don't spread yourself thin. The decisions you make today and the quality of your work will open more doors in the future. Ask yourself, what is your goal? What is your mission? Don't lose sight of that. Every decision you make reflects on your business. The trust you earn is because of who you are at your core.

4. Delegate, find talent, and listen.

As CEO, a significant challenge is to delegate. Founders and CEOs DO NOT know it all. A great leader leads with a position to understand and learn. Know your strengths, but more importantly, know your weaknesses. Fill the voids that need attention so you can grow your business.

5. Stop "networking."

Shift from networking to instilling daily kindness. The power of kindness is inexplicable. You can focus on the prize, but remember that some seeds grow in the most unexpected places. Meet those with whom you feel a shared connection, someone who you would want as your "friend." Eventually, your "friends" will inspire you and create a safe place to learn and grow.

KAY UNGER

CEO, KAY UNGER DESIGN; PRESIDENT AND CEO, KAY UNGER FAMILY FOUNDATION; CHAIR EMERITA, THE PARSONS SCHOOL OF DESIGN; EXECUTIVE BOARD, RETAILERS UNITED

Fashion designer, mentor, entrepreneur, and philanthropist Kay Unger founded and managed four global fashion companies: The Gillian Group, Kay Unger New York, Kay J's Pajamas, and Phoebe Couture. Kay created the Kay Unger Home Collection for Bed, Bath & Beyond and a successful line of Kay Unger eyewear.

Kay's service activities and honors include President of Fashion Group International, member of the Council of Fashion Designers of America, founding member of the Committee of 200, the first woman member of the Boys & Girls Club of America Board of Directors, and a recipient of the City of Hope Spirit of Life Award. Kay is a committed Trustee of the New School and a member and former Chair of the Board of the Parsons School of Design. She is also a member of the Board of the New York Stem Cell Research Foundation.

> "Collaboration comes from the heart. It is spiritual, stemming from a strong desire to help the world become a better place for men and women."

My Five Wisdoms

1. Dream big.

When I was eight years old, I got my first sewing machine; as my parents slept, I took bedspreads, turning them into skirts, robes, and things for relatives and friends. I followed my passion without knowing where it led. I never thought I could be a designer. Designers were all geniuses. I was just a girl who could create beautiful things. You, too, must dream big.

2. Women must keep working together.

We work together with many women who share my worldview. For example, I am a creative advisor for Line in the Sand, founded by Lynne Fletcher O'Brien, who devotes 100 percent of the profits to charities. She wants to protect the ocean while searching for ways to combat cancer. Work with other women to build better solutions for today's problems.

3. Collaborate with men to support women.

You will probably be working with men. Collaborate with them. Some men joined me in moving my businesses forward. Others didn't help at all. When I started, it was much harder for women without a male partner, even if her talents drove the business. I looked for the value that each male partner contributed. You should foster collaboration with men. Never let others challenge your self-confidence. I am where I am because of and despite these men.

4. Beautiful people live beautiful lives.

I have helped women my whole career by making them feel beautiful, not just through the dresses we produced but through my positive approach to everything I do. My work group was my family. In managing these incredible designers and sewers, pattern makers, and production staff, I treated them respectfully, conveying that each was an integral part of the design and production process. My purpose was to help women and men become their best selves. When they saw themselves as successful and competent, they felt beautiful happiness.

5. Give back.

I made money not just to live a rewarding life but to support my purpose and passions. Being an effective mentor, I am not responsible for the success of my mentees. Yet I have helped them realize they are talented, creative, bright, and supported. I showed them a path to self-fulfillment and self-realization. That alone can give them the strength and energy to excel. You can do the same.

"*Every conversation should be an opportunity to make an introduction to another woman.*"

—Alexandra Lebenthal

CHAPTER 7

FINANCIAL AND VENTURE TRAILBLAZERS INVESTING IN THE FUTURE

These financial trailblazers in venture capital, wealth management, and financial institutions are tackling challenges women face when seeking the right capital for their businesses. While venture capital funding in 2021 reached record levels, only 2.3 percent of VC funding went to women-owned companies. Women often take pride in growing their businesses through income and cash flows or have angel funding, bank loans, or even credit cards. The women in this chapter are trying to change these dynamics so women can get the financing they need for their businesses at the right time.

One common pattern is how women business owners confront their financing requirements and the topic of money. Often, they don't know where to go for the right guidance. At times, they find themselves overwhelmed. It is time to support these women business owners with the right education, advice, and financial counsel.

What are they sharing? First, these women tell you to listen and then listen more. Remember that what you hear may not be what someone means, so listen carefully to learn what matters. As you think about this, try to be on the leading edge of a movement, any idea, or a positive trend that can change lives. You are part of a dramatic transformation as women connect with other women to change the dynamics of business.

We are witnessing better representation of women in capital and finance, which will ultimately fuel women-led firms to reach their full economic potential. While they are experts in the world of finance, they understand the power of human potential as an important investment, as well.

As women who mean business, we salute these financially talented women who accelerate progress, profit, and identifiable, measurable results across their industries. They help us create solid platforms for businesses to succeed.

These women want to impact the numbers accelerating the pace of progress. Remember, they tell you: find your power, and never give it away. There's no time to wait.

LYNNE BORN

CHIEF PRACTICE OFFICER, ASPIRIANT

Lynne Born is Chief Practice Officer for Aspiriant, one of the nation's leading independent wealth management firms. Lynne leads all client service lines across the country, encompassing client growth, strategic planning, service delivery, and optimal resource allocation. She specializes in strategic planning, brand and business development initiatives, coaching the next generation, and succession strategies. Lynne has more than 20 years of experience in the high-net-worth space, previously as CEO, Partner, and President.

> "Always stay grounded in your 'why' and know your purpose. Mine is to help others bring their vision to life, to self-actualize themselves and their work, and to build concentric rings of positive impact by supporting individuals, families, and my community."

My Five Wisdoms

1. Support the rising generation.
Coaching next-generation leaders is personally satisfying and creates a personal and professional legacy that lives into the future. Coaching increases bonds between the generations, supports confidence, encourages autonomous thought by guiding rather than telling, and creates reverse mentoring opportunities for the more senior generation.

2. Be a strategist and an operator.
To be an effective leader in today's business environment, we need to be both strategists and operators—visionaries in touch with the overall market and business trends but also oriented with a bias toward action and execution. For business, create synergy between the external market and the internal culture by connecting the parts to the whole, seeking cohesion and integration among the people, behaviors, values, and structures that make up the entire company. Our overarching goal is to make the vision come to life!

3. Collaborate and clarify.
The business landscape—and next-generation leaders—have moved to a more collaborative and inclusive leadership style. Women excel in collaboration and inclusion! Collaboration means people are "seen and heard" and feel valued as a core part of the purpose and mission of the company.

4. Be an expert in brand differentiation for yourself and your company.
Be able to clearly and concisely identify the unique characteristics that differentiate you (and your company) from a sea of competitors. Personal and business brand differentiation is the overlooked powerhouse that, when clarified and leveraged, will exponentially fuel growth and scale for yourself and your company.

5. Remain human, and err on the side of generosity.
Create a kind and considerate culture of understanding of the personal pressures and daily challenges of life outside of work. Parents are juggling family needs, caring for aging partners, there are illnesses and deaths in the family—these are moments to pause and support each other with care and empathy, providing the time, space, care, and concern as we support each other in the journey of life.

HEATHER ETTINGER

CHAIRWOMAN, FAIRPORT WEALTH; FOUNDER, LUMA WEALTH

A champion for women and girls for over 30 years, Heather Ettinger runs a nationally recognized wealth management and holistic advisory firm. She is the bestselling author of *Lumination: Shining a Light on a Woman's Journey to Financial Wellness,* a book designed especially for women with tools and strategies to design and live more intentionally and abundantly. Heather's passion for educating and uplifting others has made her a sought-after speaker for industry associations, company women's initiatives, and wellness events. In addition, she has served on numerous nonprofit and corporate boards, primarily in health care, financial services, and consumer products.

> "Having control over your time and options is becoming one of the most valuable currencies in the world. Take clarity breaks to focus on your priorities."

My Five Wisdoms

1. Design your roadmap.

Do the work to find your own unique path. Read *Lumination: Shining a Light on a Woman's Journey to Financial Wellness* to reflect on your past and present so that you can design a more intentional future. Revisit it every year to reassess if you need to course correct.

2. Stop bushwhacking!

Staying on your path takes work. When you say yes, what are you saying no to? You didn't just get more hours in your day. Women too often are so busy that they don't pause to reflect on the highest and best use of their time. I take 24 to 48 hours to review a request before responding to assess if it aligns with my priorities. Develop a "quit list" of those things that take you offtrack monthly.

3. Trail guides are essential.

Develop your personal advisory board to guide you through life and career crossroads. Who can support you but also bring a different perspective? Who will cheer for you, run through walls for you, and call you on your blind spots? Different paths and detours may require new advisors to be added. Create intentional connection and community with those who are important to you, care for you, challenge, teach, and help show you the way. Men are great, but your girlfriends will get you through life!

4. Be prepared for bad financial weather, roadblocks, and the long haul.

Money self-care is smart care. Optimal health and optimal wealth are not separable. The largest source of stress in this country is financial. Take steps to find resources and advisors who will help you build your financial roadmap personally and professionally.

5. Lift as you climb. "Shine on."

How can you pay it forward and help other women and girls? How can you open a door, mentor, coach, and advise others who might need guidance and to hear how you navigated similar challenges and opportunities? Shine a light on their path and you might learn something new about yourself on the journey!

JUDITH GOLDKRAND

SENIOR VICE PRESIDENT, THE NATIONAL WOMEN'S SEGMENT LEADER, NATIONAL LGBTQ+ SEGMENT LEADER, WELLS FARGO

Judith Goldkrand is a passionate advocate for women, an experienced banker, board member, philanthropist, builder of high-performing teams, and creator of psychological safety in the workplace. Her goal is to change the world for women. Judith dedicates herself to the advancement of women, gender equity, access to capital for women, and empowering others to use their voices. Judith is a mentor for women entrepreneurs on growth and capital. She also sponsors women in the corporate workplace in their career development. Judith is currently the National Women's Segment Leader and National LGBTQ+ Segment Leader at Wells Fargo.

> "Be generous, kind, and open. Listen with a whole heart. Care deeply about others. Share your connections, network, and resources. Make an impact every day."

My Five Wisdoms

1. Ask questions.

It is always OK not to know. What is not OK is not to ask. Help is available, and you do not have to do everything alone. Find a network of trusted advisors and leverage their knowledge. Stay curious and be willing to learn all the time.

2. Believe in yourself.

You are worth it. Own your ideas and stand up for yourself. Trust yourself and be open to learning and growth. Create positive affirmations to replace negative head chatter. Never give up on yourself. Be strong and have courage.

3. Learn the rules of the game.

Do the work. Educate yourself. Show up every day to make a difference. Learn from good examples and those you would not repeat. Do not be afraid to make a mistake. Surround yourself with experts, and become confident in the knowledge yourself.

4. Let people know they matter and belong.

Care about others. Create a safe environment of equity and inclusion: a place where all belong and matter for who they are as their authentic selves. Listen generously and be empathetic. Make spaces for all voices in the room because this is where creativity and life will thrive.

5. Build community.

There is value in community, in being together, sharing ideas, knowledge, and experiences, mentoring, and caring. When we collaborate and work together, we grow more effectively, faster, and elevate each other. Reach out early and often. Know your community is there for you even when you are not there for yourself.

JILL JOHNSON

COFOUNDER AND CEO, INSTITUTE FOR ENTREPRENEURIAL LEADERSHIP

Jill Johnson is a nationally recognized thought leader and trailblazer working to foster an inclusive entrepreneurial ecosystem. Jill is the Cofounder and CEO of the Institute for Entrepreneurial Leadership (IFEL), a nonprofit that works to eradicate the barriers that prevent entrepreneurs from historically excluded populations from building personal and community wealth through entrepreneurship. Jill spearheads innovative programming to address the systemic barriers faced by entrepreneurs of color. Her superpower is connecting the dots. Jill has a BA in economics from Harvard University and is married with four amazing sons.

> "Don't wait to have leadership opportunities bestowed upon you. Figure out what needs to be changed, and lead the charge."

My Five Wisdoms

1. Lean into your superpower.

We all have gifts and talents, but your super-power is that attribute that comes naturally to you. It's what you love doing, it gives you energy when you share it, and there is a benefit to others when you exercise it. It is not always easy to recognize, but when you do, you will unlock your genius and be unstoppable.

2. Act with fearlessness.

There is a difference between being fearless and acting with fearlessness. When we understand that there will be situations that cause us to feel fear throughout our lifetime, it gives us the license to acknowledge how we feel and to recognize that the decision that we face in the moment is how to act despite the fear. Choosing to act with fearlessness helps us overcome barriers of the mind and pushes us to our greatest potential.

3. Keep your finances in focus and in your control.

It's easy to get swept up in your passions and forget that you must maintain a certain income to pay for your lifestyle. Whether you are a business owner or are climbing the career ladder, know how much income you need to cover your current and future living expenses. If you are married or in a long-term relationship, keep control of your finances so you can have peace of mind regardless of how the relationship develops.

4. Identify your triggers.

Each of us has people, places, and situations that can kill our mood and sometimes send us into a dark place. Be introspective to understand what those are and figure out your strategies for how to minimize the frequency of the triggering occurrences.

5. Create three energy boosters.

Happiness is key to keeping the lows in check. It could be a favorite coffee beverage, a scenic location, a song, or salsa dancing . . . figure out what lifts you and helps you live with joy. Everything in life isn't fun and games, but if you plan regular time for doing the small things that make you smile, life feels much more enjoyable.

ALEXANDRA JUNG

COFOUNDER AND MANAGING PARTNER, AMATERAS CAPITAL; HEAD OF PRIVATE DEBT, AEA INVESTORS

Alexandra Jung has over 28 years of experience in the investment industry as an investor and business leader across the U.S. and European markets. She recently founded Amateras Capital, a private credit and equity investment firm. Prior to Amateras, Alex was a Partner and Head of Europe at Oak Hill Advisors, a U.S.-based $50 billion investment firm. She is an experienced corporate board director and currently serves on the board of NVR, Inc., and its Audit Committee. Before joining Oak Hill Advisors, Alex managed investments in credit, distressed debt, and equity as part of Goldman Sachs & Co.'s Special Situations Group and at Greywolf Capital. In addition, Alex worked at Houlihan Lokey Howard & Zukin in the Financial Restructuring Group. Alex serves on the Board of Trustees of Bucknell University, on the investment and finance committee, and as a founding member of the Women Business Collaborative. She earned a master of management from the J.L. Kellogg Graduate School of Management at Northwestern University and a BA, cum laude, from Bucknell University. She is passionate about promoting diversity in the investment industry and across business leadership as a driver of business value creation.

> "Fight for the things you care about, but do it in a way that will lead others to join you."
>
> —Ruth Bader Ginsburg

My Five Wisdoms

1. Embrace opportunity and change.

Don't overthink and talk yourself out of the next challenge. Ask for that promotion, next role, etc. My group was building a London business early in my career at Goldman Sachs. When I asked my boss to be considered, he was shocked and said, "But what would your husband say? You just got married." That London role set me up for a later role as a Partner, leading and building the European business for a growing and prominent investment firm.

2. Ask for help.

We think we must do it all on our own, but there are so many resources and people out there who have navigated similar challenges. Just ASK for advice, guidance, etc. People like talking about their experiences, and those perspectives are incredibly valuable.

3. Lead—be that role model.

Even if you don't realize it, the next generation of all genders is paying attention. Women leaders can be multipliers of impact by showing younger women the path to leadership and success. We founded Amateras Capital to show the power of leveraging women's investment and operating executives to create business value.

4. Inspire and be inspired.

Surround yourself with people, places, and activities that inspire you. Get involved in organizations that inspire you. Find physical places where you can find inspiration—for me, it's the ocean. The place where you can recharge and find your energy and focus. Positive energy is a force and being around it and exuding it are empowering.

5. Empower others.

Nothing is more fulfilling than helping someone achieve a goal and finding little and big ways you can impact someone's life. It's amazing to see the power of women helping women.

SHELLY KAPOOR COLLINS

INVESTMENT PARTNER, SWAY VENTURES

Shelly Kapoor Collins is an Investment Partner at Sway Ventures, where she leads early-stage investing in technology companies founded by women and diverse founders. Before Sway, Shelly founded the Shatter Fund and established it as the premier brand investing in technology companies led and started by female entrepreneurs. Shelly is investing at Sway Ventures with the same focus to drive an inclusive innovation economy.

Before founding Shatter, Shelly was appointed to the National Women's Business Council (NWBC) in the second Obama administration and served as Vice Chair of the Women in Public Service Project started by Secretary Hillary Clinton while at the State Department. Shelly served on the transition team for then-Attorney General Kamala D. Harris and was a Founding Member of the NFC for the presidential campaign for then-Senator Harris. Shelly previously served as a National Co-Chair for Technology for Barack Obama's 2012 presidential campaign.

Shelly is an Honorary Friend of the U.S. Department of State's U.S.–India Alliance. Shelly has been named one of the Top 20 Global Influential Indian women by the *Economic Times of India* and was named to *Forbes*'s "40 Women to Watch Over 40" list.

> "Pick your timing, and do not wait to be asked. With the multiple hats women wear, there is never the right time to start one's own business."

My Five Wisdoms

1. Women need to be door openers, not gatekeepers for other women.
Our collective power is what makes us strongest.

2. Pay it forward without any expectations, because that's when the magic happens.
Transactional relationships do not go the distance.

3. Get out of your comfort zone.
Say YES to doing something new because it could become one of the most pivotal moments of your life. A unique opportunity, an introductory meeting, a volunteer role: say YES.

4. Put yourself out there.
You cannot accomplish anything sitting at home. If you don't know anyone in a room, always find another woman and stand with her.

5. No matter how tough the path, do NOT stop.
Keep going because you will eventually reach your goal, maybe even better than you expected.

KAY KOPLOVITZ

COFOUNDER AND CHAIRMAN, SPRINGBOARD ENTERPRISES; FOUNDER, USA NETWORK

Kay Koplovitz is Cofounder and Chairman of Springboard Enterprises, a nonprofit 501(c)(3) accelerator that trains women-led entrepreneurs of technology and life sciences companies to raise capital. Kay is the Founder and former CEO of USA Network and the Syfy Channel (formerly Sci-Fi Channel), today a multibillion-dollar cable television network under NBCU. She ran the network for 21 years before stepping down in 1998, selling it for $4.5 billion. As Founder of USA Network, Kay is the visionary who created the business model for cable networks by introducing the concept of two revenue streams: licensing and advertising.

> "The serendipitous moment of hearing an Arthur C. Clarke lecture focused my passion on launching a television network delivered by satellite, and USA Network was born."

My Five Wisdoms

1. Build your network.

You may remember the saying, "Build a well before you need a drink of water." Same with a network of experts and advisors. Build your network while building your company or your career. Offer to help an expert and build a relationship you can return to later for advice and connections.

2. Build a great team with experts you don't have.

Hire and surround yourself with people who are more knowledgeable than you are in their areas of expertise, and empower them to achieve your vision. A founder is much like an orchestra conductor who plays no instrument but must produce a perfect performance.

3. Let team members take risks.

Building a great company takes teamwork, transparency, and trust. Three Ts that will propel you a long way. Almost nothing inspires a team member more who has raised their hand to take a shot at something than believing that you have trust in their ability to perform.

4. Think fast and act.

Thinking fast and acting fast are very different than thinking fast and acting slow, but you often must be creative and act in real time. When I was first building USA Network into a sports powerhouse, I signed a contract with George Steinbrenner to broadcast the Yankees games. After the first game televised in 1979, I got a call from Bowie Kuhn, Commissioner of Major League Baseball. He told me that I had to drop the games or he would take me to court. His reason? Steinbrenner didn't have the right to sell them. Gulp. After a series of calls that day, it struck me that I had one last play. I told him I would trade him my Yankees contract for one with Major League Baseball. That did it! A worthless contract turned into a baseball powerhouse!

5. Philosophy: win-win.

My approach to business has always been win-win. Others practice I win-you lose. One of the best pieces of advice I received from one mentor, Bob Rosencrans, was to leave something on the table for others to have some win too. It builds relationships.

ALEXANDRA LEBENTHAL

SENIOR ADVISOR, HOULIHAN LOKEY

Alexandra Lebenthal is a Senior Advisor at Houlihan Lokey, where she leads an initiative focused on female-led companies. Previously, Alexandra was CEO of Lebenthal Holdings, a municipal bond firm founded by her grandparents in 1925. After its sale, Alexandra restarted the firm and ran it until 2017. Alexandra has been frequently recognized as a leader and champion for women in business. She was named one of New York's "100 Most Influential Women" by *Crain's New York Business* in 1999, one of the "Top 50 Women in Wealth Management" by *Wealth Manager* in 2009, listed in *Crain*'s "Largest Women-Owned Businesses" and "Fast 50" lists in 2013, and received an Honorable Mention in "Most Influential Women in Mid-Market M&A" in 2022.

A graduate of Princeton University, she is the NYC Vice Chair of C200, the leading organization for women in business; Board Member of Graf Acquisition; and Advisory Board Member of InterPrice Technologies, Inc.

> "If you have been privileged to get in the room before other women who deserve to be there, stick your high heel in the door and leave it open for everyone else. The room is big enough for everyone."

My Five Wisdoms

1. Be a part of the ever-unfolding fabric of women connecting with one another.
Every conversation should be an opportunity to make an introduction to another woman.

2. Don't set yourself up to feel like you haven't been able to find balance.
Balance isn't getting to one point where it's all smooth sailing going forward. There are days when you feel like a failure, as well as those days when you get it all done right. Recognize that, and you can let go of the unattainable.

3. Meet everyone!
I think of how many meaningful relationships and opportunities came from one conversation, one cup of coffee, or one event. I may not have thought it was important, or sometimes even of value at the time, but looking back, I realize the stepping stones that have led me to where I am today.

4. A bump in the road may be an opportunity to get off the highway.
Rather than looking at mistakes as failures, they are moments to think about where you want to be and make a choice to find a new road in a new car. It may be a little extra bumpy for a while, but it also takes you to a new place where you were meant to be.

5. Don't be afraid to talk about your failures.
Everyone has moments in life when they mess something up. Most people are reticent to talk about it, but those are the things that make you real and relatable and show that it happens to even the seemingly most successful.

LORETTA McCARTHY

CO-CEO AND MANAGING PARTNER, GOLDEN SEEDS

Loretta McCarthy is Co-CEO and Managing Partner of Golden Seeds, an investment organization that invests in early-stage, women-led companies in the United States. Golden Seeds is one of the country's largest and most active angel investment networks. The organization is recognized as a leader in the movement to fund women entrepreneurs and for its advocacy of women entrepreneurs, gender diversity, and the education of angel investors. Loretta has been a lifelong advocate of women, repeatedly using her skills and interests on behalf of women—in business, sports, politics, justice, and life.

> "The success of every woman should be the inspiration to another. We should raise each other up."
>
> —Serena Williams

My Five Wisdoms

1. Be on the leading edge of a movement, an idea, or a positive trend that can change lives.

I have had the good fortune of leading mission-driven organizations, creating lasting impact that changes the world and provides immense satisfaction for my colleagues and me. Golden Seeds is a great example. We set out to change the landscape of early-stage investing by funding only women-led companies—creating measurable, lasting, and palpable impact.

2. Embrace your own power.

Women have phenomenal power, but do you realize or value yours? The sooner we grasp our power, the sooner we will lead with purpose, confidence, intention, and joy. Seek the support of organizations such as Take the Lead, which offers excellent programs that can accelerate your path to realizing your power. The Founder of Take the Lead, Gloria Feldt, commented, "This post-pandemic time is the moment when a quantum leap to gender parity in pay, position, and power can occur."

3. Listen—and then listen some more.

I have spent much of my career in marketing roles, which many people think of as communications. True, but all effective communications start with listening to customers, employees, competitors, and research. And I mean really listening, particularly to those who don't share your views. Listening and hearing what is said is as accurate for internal conversations as for external communications and life in general.

4. Pay it forward.

There are countless ways to support other women. Be intentional about this. Sign up to be a mentor, sponsor the growth of women, or participate in organizations that focus on the advancement of women. Above all, be alert to opportunities, and don't wait to be asked.

5. Take stock.

Find time to assess your satisfaction with your choices. Enjoy the gratification of pursuing passions, continuing to learn, broadening horizons, and finding time for yourself. In the enduring words of Mae West, "You only live once, but if you do it right, once is enough."

KIM MOORE

PARTNER, VENTURE CAPITAL TEAM,
GLYNN CAPITAL

Kim Moore is a Partner on the Venture Capital Team at Glynn Capital. Kim is passionate about building companies, adding immediate value to businesses during their inflection point, and connecting people in meaningful ways to succeed on two fronts: business development engagements and building diverse leadership teams and boards. Previously, she was at Innovation Endeavors, an early-stage venture capital firm solely backed by Eric Schmidt. Prior to working in venture capital, Kim worked at Asana. Kim received her undergraduate degree with honors in social science from the University of California, Irvine, and her EdM from Harvard Graduate School of Education.

> "I would not be in my position today if others did not believe in me. It just takes one person to elevate you. Be that person for someone else. Be the change-maker."

My Five Wisdoms

1. Build your network ASAP.
Start building your network. Be intentional regarding who you want to meet and stay in touch with. You will be new to the scene, but don't worry. Try to follow up with someone in a way that adds value. This touch can be small and straightforward, like, "Here's an interesting article or a cool event happening I thought you would be interested in."

2. Help others.
Please pay it forward to others who were in your shoes. The future depends on you to help bring others to the top. Be mindful of those that might not be in the spotlight but who should be—champion deserving people. Celebrate small and big wins, both privately and publicly.

3. Practice your craft.
Start early and learn the skills you need regardless of your job title. If you want to work for an investment firm, make sure you understand how to articulate what makes your investing style unique or value-additive to that firm you want to work for.

4. Do your homework and prep before you meet with someone.
Come prepared with what goals you have and how you can help them. End the meeting with, "By the way, how can I be helpful to you?"

5. Define your expertise and refine your brand.
As you grow in your career, be known as an expert in something. Create a brand around this so that people know what they can come to you for and remember you.

RACHEL VINSON

PRESIDENT, DEBT & STRUCTURED FINANCE
IN THE UNITED STATES, CBRE

Rachel Vinson leads CBRE's Debt & Structured Finance business in the United States. Previously, she was the Global Chief Operating Officer of CBRE Global Capital Markets. Rachel has more than 20 years of experience in real estate and financial services. She served as Senior Vice President and Head of Finance for CBRE's Americas Advisory business segment, overseeing financial support and business partnering across all Advisory lines of business. Before joining CBRE, Rachel spent six years with Barings Multifamily Capital, LLC, where she was elevated to President, overseeing strategic direction and operations for the debt origination and servicing company.

> "Enjoy the journey. Yours is one of a kind. Have the confidence and faith to embrace each step, knowing today is preparing you for tomorrow."

My Five Wisdoms

1. Declare your affirmations each day.
Say three to five positive affirmations daily. Say them out loud, as you mean it, even if you may not believe it. The words you say to yourself will eventually play out in your actions and shape not only how you view yourself but how others view you.

2. Find your power, and don't give it away.
Emotional intelligence is critical. Focus on what you can control. Learn to identify what really matters. Everything else is noise. The moment you get caught up in the "noise," you start giving away your power.

3. Use self-qualifiers and self-promotion with confidence.
People know what you allow them to know about you. Don't wait for someone to realize your capabilities. You must tell them. Using self-qualifiers and self-promotion is an excellent way to do this. Here's an example of how to respond when asked for a suggestion on how to solve an issue: "When I was in my last role as the head of sales, I approached a similar issue by first identifying the underlying communication gap. Because I took this approach, we could implement a solution quickly." You confidently qualified as an experienced professional whose opinion matters, and you promoted your experience. You just set your own narrative for others to repeat.

4. Stop apologizing!
Ask yourself, "Did I do anything wrong?" The goal is not perfection. The goal is to grow continually. Challenge yourself to replace "I'm sorry" with "thank you." When someone follows up on an email that you haven't had a chance to respond to, begin by saying, "Thank you for the follow-up," versus "I'm sorry for the slow reply."

5. Get a coach. Be a coach.
You don't have to be superwoman, and you don't have to go it alone. It's not just about paving the path for the next woman behind you. It's about bringing other women beside you along. Embrace the resources, networks, advocates, mentors, and coaches around you. Realize that men and women want to learn from you and your unique experience.

"Lift as you climb. Women must support and encourage each other! . . . Bring someone with you. . . . Help open the door for someone else."

—Sandra Quince

CHAPTER 8

WOMEN ORGANIZATION CEOS
PROPELLING PROGRESS

The women in this chapter are leading organizations focused on helping women at all levels of business, from those early-stage entrepreneurs to those pursuing careers in large companies. They know we must change the culture of corporations, not just advocate for the women in those organizations.

These association leaders understand the importance of collaboration. These women are part of a more significant movement wherein each community values what the others are doing. They must work together to achieve meaningful results for the greater good of womanhood.

Their organizations have agendas ranging from holding governments accountable to compliance regulations to raising and improving women's standards at work. Fundamental is pursuing parity, gender equality, and women's empowerment. They are developing programs, capturing the data, and building allies, all to accelerate change where it is needed now. They exemplify how we are stronger together.

These women bring a unique perspective on the alignment of corporate culture to talent strategy and business results. Some urge you to build those inclusive workplaces that thrive on the style and skills of women leaders. They have learned through their careers to build on their optimism. These women are tackling outdated cultural standards, along with the laws and the challenges women face, from work to family to life. They have risen from a need, a calling, and a purpose, assembled to impact society and create a better world for us all. These women show us the business of women at its very best. They remind us to face the challenges of tomorrow with positive energy and laser-sharp focus.

ESTHER AGUILERA

PRESIDENT AND CEO, LATINO CORPORATE DIRECTORS ASSOCIATION (LCDA)

Esther Aguilera is President and CEO of the Latino Corporate Directors Association (LCDA), where she brings together accomplished executives to advance diversity in the boardroom. She is a corporate governance expert and executive producer of the LCDA Board Leaders Convening. Esther contributes corporate governance, ESG, and DEI expertise serving on the Advisory Council of the NACD Center for Inclusive Governance, the Board of Directors of the Thirty Percent Coalition, and the Board of Advisors of the Latinx Executive Alliance, as well as serving as an advisor to other leading organizations. She received the Alumni Seal Award for Service to the Community from her alma mater, Occidental College. She's been recognized as the 2021 Person of the Year by Al Día News Media, one of ALPFA's 2021 50 Most Powerful Latinas, and one of *Hispanic Executive*'s 2021 Top Ten Líderes, among others.

> "What ends up happening is that you're setting up winners and losers: if there is only a focus on gender, Latinos and African Americans lose out."

My Five Wisdoms

1. Find great teachers, and follow their wisdom.

Growing up, I was fortunate to have teachers who supported me, helped me understand the value of education, and propelled me to my career. I listened, learned, and appreciated their wisdom. Find your teacher and hear what they are saying.

2. Embrace the challenges of the future.

My second wisdom is that you embrace change and don't flee a challenge. I grew up in Los Angeles and didn't know any other place. I got invited to work at an organization in Washington, DC. I had good advisors who encouraged me as I made the leap of faith that this was good for my future. Success comes in unexpected ways. Embrace opportunities as part of your emerging future.

3. The unknown in front of you can become the best experience.

Don't be afraid of new uncomfortable places, because that's how you grow, learn, and broaden your horizons. Whether it is a new position or a new place to live, you must tackle the uncertainties before you.

4. Who is with you on your journey?

Surround yourself with folks that are in your corner. When you might feel like you don't have what it takes, they are there to encourage you. Everyone goes through that at different stages in different phases. Build your team with good people and good mentors.

5. Put yourself out there for new opportunities. Raise your hand.

I learned this when I did not apply for a position that was perfect for me. Then someone said, "Why haven't you applied?" My lesson learned was that it's OK to put yourself out there. Don't be too timid or wait to be asked. Culturally, Latinas are told, "Who do you think you are to put yourself out there or aspire to X, Y, and Z," and that holds you back. Don't let anything hold you back. Be bold and brave.

SUBHA V. BARRY

PRESIDENT, SERAMOUNT

Subha V. Barry is a C-suite leader who brings a unique perspective on the alignment of corporate culture to talent strategy and business results. She is President of Seramount, part of EAB, a strategic professional services and research firm dedicated to advancing diversity, equity, and inclusion in the workplace. Before Seramount, Subha was Senior Vice President and Chief Diversity Officer at Freddie Mac. She also spent 20-plus years at Merrill Lynch as Managing Director and the company's first Global Head of Diversity and Inclusion. She is a transformational change agent who speaks passionately about driving innovation by embracing diversity, equity, and inclusion. Subha serves on several boards.

> "Intersectional allyship will require us to be teachers of some and students of others, bold and vulnerable in asking for help. Be laser-focused on the goal of creating equity."

My Five Wisdoms

1. Learn the value of gaining profit and loss (P&L) responsibility early in your career.

We at Seramount believe this experience is critical in advancing to the C-suite. The most surprising findings from our 2019 study, "The Gender Gap at the Top," are that many women don't know what career paths they need to get to the top, don't understand the importance of relationships with mentors and sponsors, and are not encouraged to take on revenue-generating (P&L) jobs that are often required for the highest levels of corporate America.

2. Learn to listen. You have two ears and one mouth for a reason.

Not having all the answers is OK. It took me a little while to learn this. Know what you don't know, and don't be afraid to ask questions along the way. Take risks, and don't be afraid to fail. "You win or you learn" should be your mantra.

3. Learn. Do. Teach.

When you are good at something, take the time to teach someone else that skill set. Lead with a spirit of generosity, and assume that people come from a place of good intentions.

Also, think about whether you are actively seeking allies, both men and women, within your organization. If you are a leader within your organization, think about those you have looked out for, mentored, or advocated for. Watch out for these high-potential women, nurture them, and help them succeed.

4. Know yourself.

Can you look at yourself in the mirror and acknowledge the "whole" you? Faults and all? To do that, you have to know your strengths and weaknesses, your triggers and your inspirations. Once you know that and embrace it, you will know how to act and behave in a variety of circumstances and environments. You know when to be bold and speak up and when to be quiet, observant, and introspective.

5. Figure out your superpower.

Each of us brings a unique skill set to our organizations. Ask yourself: What am I good at? And once you figure that out, can you match it to the business of what your company does? Be the best you can be, and make sure you are getting joy from doing it.

LORRAINE HARITON

PRESIDENT AND CEO, CATALYST

Lorraine Hariton is President and CEO of Catalyst, a global nonprofit work-ing with the world's most powerful CEOs and leading companies to build workplaces that work for women. Catalyst's vision and mission are to accelerate progress for women through workplace inclusion. This lifelong passion for Lorraine has helped her build a career with senior-level positions in Silicon Valley as an entrepreneur and executive. Beginning at IBM, Lorraine has served in the Obama administration at the Department of State and developed the Global STEM Alliance at the New York Academy of Sciences. She has served on the UN Women Global Innovation Coalition for Change boards, the Clayman Institute for Gender Research at Stanford University, and the Forum for Entrepreneurs and Executives.

Lorraine holds a bachelor of science degree in mathematical sciences from Stanford University and a master of business administration degree from Harvard Business School.

> "Throughout my life, I've navigated dyslexia academically and professionally, leading me to a guiding principle: Major your majors. Nurture your unique gifts."

My Five Wisdoms

1. Create sponsorship programs to help make women more visible as leaders, because relationships matter.

As a woman entering the workforce in the mid-1970s, I started my career in tech when few people looked like me. I was lucky to have sponsors who encouraged me, helping me get to where I am. These sponsors were also models for how to help others.

2. Advocate for the future of work, and make flexible work options available to working women.

Leaders must meet this transformative moment in the future of work—when so many workers are reevaluating their work-life priorities—by letting go of the old workplace models and reimagining a more humane workplace. It's good for women and suitable for everyone.

3. Garner buy-in and true partnership from men across all levels of the organization.

Build a culture of gender partnership in which people of all genders work together to advance gender equity. The work of reimagining the workplace is not women's work alone.

4. Amplify success stories and provide role models for women working their way up through the pipeline.

As a woman who can sponsor other women and as the leader of a global organization advancing women in the workplace more broadly, I take these roles seriously, elevating women and accelerating the progress toward equitable, empathic leadership.

5. Build inclusive workplaces with empathy at the center of all you do.

Leaders must engage their teams and colleagues with curiosity, humility, courage, allyship, ownership, and accountability. Shift the onus from individual women to our larger systems, placing the responsibility on workplaces to evolve.

ANNA MOK

PRESIDENT AND EXECUTIVE BOARD CHAIR, ASCEND AND ASCEND FOUNDATION; COFOUNDER, ASCEND PINNACLE

Anna Mok is a Senior Partner at Deloitte & Touche LLP, where she is the Private Equity Leader and the Asia Pacific Leader for the Advisory Practice. She is also President, Executive Chairperson and Cofounder of Ascend, North America's premier organization of Pan-Asian business professionals. She inspires others to make positive, sustained workplace and societal impacts and is a passionate advocate for underrepresented professionals. Anna was the first Chinese American woman admitted to partnership at Deloitte, serving as a member of Deloitte's Board Council, the CEO Advisory Partner Council, and Advisory's Executive Committee. She serves on the boards of The Conference Board, Commonwealth Club of California, United Way Bay Area, and Thirty Percent Coalition and on multiple corporate advisory councils.

> "Embrace and don't run away from what's new, unknown, or undefined. It has never led me wrong to view these as opportunities to build and create something unique and special!"

My Five Wisdoms

1. Be generous with your capital.

And I don't mean just financial capital (though it's good to share that too!). Your time, friendship, counsel, advocacy, and service to others are all different forms of "capital" you have that can be gifted to others. From my own experience, I've learned that anytime I am generous, I am the biggest beneficiary in ways that ultimately enrich and give fuller meaning to my life.

2. Create your own "Success Compass."

While others can inspire and be role models for us, we ultimately must define what success means by charting our path forward. This starts with us knowing and owning our strengths and frailties, accepting who we are with all our human complexities, and at the same time allowing ourselves to evolve and blossom. Only by seeing ourselves clearly and accepting our potential and pitfalls can we establish our own "true north."

3. Allow yourself to wander and enjoy the journey.

When you have established your "true north," don't be afraid to wander along the way. It's less about the destination and everything about the journey. There is a whole world awaiting your discovery between where you are and where you think you want to go. Discovery is one of the true marvels of being human!

4. Set a high bar, and bring people along.

Don't be afraid of setting a high bar. You may be a visionary who sees things in the future. It can be frustrating when others aren't moving at your pace. Don't compromise your standards and goals, but give space for others to adopt your vision.

5. Adopt and embrace and-and, not either-or.

Much of our society seems to be based on a zero-sum narrative that your win is my loss or vice versa. Please don't believe it. This thinking keeps us in fear and perpetuates selfishness and negates collaboration. Women know how to collaborate. Come up with more creative ways to expand the pie for everyone.

IRENE NATIVIDAD

PRESIDENT, GLOBEWOMEN RESEARCH & EDUCATION INSTITUTE

President of GlobeWomen Research & Education Institute, Irene Natividad has convened women leaders for 33 years at the Global Summit of Women on women's economic progress; conducts research on women directors globally through Corporate Women Directors International; presents women CEOs to students through Legacies of Women; and integrates economic equity issues internationally at the Organization for Economic Co-operation and Development, Asia-Pacific Economic Cooperation (APEC), and UN meetings. Irene was the first Asian American woman to lead a U.S. political organization when she was elected Chair of the National Women's Political Caucus (1985). Recognitions include being awarded Legion d'Honneur by President of France Emmanuel Macron (2021) for her global work and "100 Most Powerful Women in America" by *Ladies' Home Journal.*

> "I want women to have money because money is power, and women have little of both globally."

My Five Wisdoms

1. Stay true to who you are, no matter what you decide to do in life.

We all have a work persona that often does not match our "real" selves, like the jacket we wear over leggings for Zoom calls. This disparity causes stress because it requires some measure of trust and a sense of belonging so that we can come out of our comfort zone and connect with people in our authentic selves.

2. Work on expanding your knowledge of people and the world because changes are happening so fast, and you don't want to be left behind.

Lifelong learning is a must, given that technological changes, market shifts, and socio/political events are accelerating. A successful professional is perennially curious, even about things that have no seeming connection to what we do.

3. As you climb up the ladder and meet success, don't forget to pull up someone else behind you.

Women are still not in charge in every arena of public life. We won't get to parity unless we pull each other along. We learn best from each other, so be a mentor to someone.

4. Know that people measure you the moment you enter a room by how you look, even before you utter a word.

This is still especially true of women, as any woman achiever will attest, so remember this truism the next time you go to an important meeting, even on Zoom.

5. You must work at being a happy person. Those who succeed tend to be optimists.

"Imagine success" someone told me, and given the ups and downs of life and careers, good mental health requires not sinking to pessimism but keeping focused and positive.

PAMELA PRINCE-EASON

PRESIDENT AND CEO, WOMEN'S BUSINESS ENTERPRISE NATIONAL COUNCIL (WBENC)

Pamela Prince-Eason is President and CEO of the Women's Business Enterprise National Council (WBENC), where she champions the "breaking down of barriers" that impact women-owned businesses wishing to compete for opportunities with corporate America and the federal government.

Her experience as a co-owner of a business and her corporate leadership makes her uniquely qualified to champion the advancement of women. In her third term as an appointee to the National Women's Business Council (NWBC), Pamela uses her voice to champion women business owners through advice, research, and policy recommendations to the United States Small Business Administration (SBA), Congress, and the president.

> "Leaders must use their voice! It is no longer acceptable for a LEADER to stand on the sidelines and remain silent on matters of great importance."

My Five Wisdoms

1. Listen with empathy for understanding, and "treat others as you would have them treat you."

Unconscious bias or predetermined thoughts and established practices limit real progress in both professional and personal life. Listening to all for understanding makes me better able to make a difference each day.

2. One person does nothing brilliant.

I believe in the strength of a TEAM. We are more intelligent, stronger, and better together, significantly when we recognize the value of each person's "unique" contributions. This collaborative teamwork leads to outcomes beyond the impact of one person alone.

3. Recognize that we all need mentors and advisors.

I learn something every day from people in my professional and personal life. It is my responsibility to ensure I seek advice from others as I continue to grow to be the best leader and person I can be.

4. Realize that each person can reach, teach, and motivate others.

Recognize that it is our responsibility to do this. The future must know the past. Yet we must pass on what we see as we motivate others to make the most significant impact they can drive.

5. Understand the economic impact of full inclusion of all people and all ideas.

WBENC serves all women and strives to impact communities by investing in women. Research shows that women business leaders invest significantly in others and their communities. A key to lifting all societies is to invest in the advancement of women and women-owned businesses.

SANDRA QUINCE

CEO, PARADIGM FOR PARITY

Sandra Quince is the CEO of Paradigm for Parity, an organization focused on achieving gender parity in the workplace. Sandra has over 15 years of experience in diversity and inclusion, talent management, and development and learning across multiple organizations and industries.

Selected as one of 50 Black women for the Goldman Sachs One Million Black Women Impact Grant, Sandra was named one of 2022's most inspiring diversity and inclusion leaders and the *Journal Record*'s 2021 "50 Making a Difference" list of honorees in Oklahoma.

> "Be a leader who creates an environment where everyone can bring their best selves and thrive! I love the quote by Mahatma Gandhi, 'The greatness of humanity is not in being human but in being humane.'"

My Five Wisdoms

1. Understand that you own your career 100 percent.

While your manager is there to guide and support your career goals and choices, you must manage your career fully. Know your worth and the value you bring to the organization and be able to articulate in meetings with your manager and senior leaders. I set aside time each year to assess my career goals to determine if I am fit in the role, ready to be broadened, or prepared for a new position.

2. Nail the core, and become a continuous learner.

You must excel in the role you are hired to execute. Having conversations with your manager about your career is critical. Don't be afraid to ask what exceeding performance looks like, and track your progress along the way. When I became CEO of Paradigm for Parity, I researched what makes CEOs successful. I discovered that most CEOs are successful because they are continuous learners. I challenge you: become continuous learners.

3. Develop and maintain a strong network.

While this does not come naturally to everyone, and it did not work for me, it is necessary! It is essential to have others who can validate you and your work. Be strategic in your networking, and know your organization's players internally and externally. Internally, networks can become sponsors and be a catalyst in your career growth. Externally, networks can function as your "board of directors," providing insight and objective feedback.

4. Lift as you climb.

Women must support and encourage each other! As you climb up the corporate ladder, don't forget to bring someone with you. Become a mentor for others or, better yet, become a sponsor and leverage your personal and professional capital to help open the door for someone else.

5. Join Paradigm for Parity.

P4P partners with organizations to achieve gender parity, including racial equity. We are dedicated to ensuring that women of all races, cultures, and backgrounds are represented at all levels of corporate leadership.

DR. ROSINA L. RACIOPPI

PRESIDENT AND CEO, WOMEN UNLIMITED, INC.

Dr. Rosina L. Racioppi is President and CEO of WOMEN Unlimited, Inc. (WUI), providing resources to corporations that support developing, retaining, and advancing female leaders. Before WUI, Rosina held executive positions in human resources in various industries.

Rosina earned her doctorate and master's degrees in education from the University of Pennsylvania. Her dissertation, "Women's Mentoring Wisdom," focused on how women effectively use mentoring at the mid-career level.

Rosina serves on the Advisory Council for the University of Pennsylvania CLO Alumni Network and the Advisory Board of The New Historia. She co-chairs the Women in the Pipeline Action Initiative for the Women Business Collaborative.

> "Find your career joy. I am passionate about helping women find careers that leverage their skills and expertise, where they can thrive."

My Five Wisdoms

1. Build relationships that matter.

Early in my career, I realized the importance of establishing relationships with people different from me—different roles, departments, or cultures. The power of these relationships informed my thinking, broadened my perspective, and provided me with guidance for my career.

2. Get specific feedback and guidance.

Women often fail to receive valuable feedback that helps prepare them for future roles. Often managers do not give specific feedback that helps women know where to shift behaviors and build new skills. Women must gain comfort in asking for helpful feedback. Using two simple questions at the end of an assignment can provide valuable insight: (1) Which area of my work stood out as valuable? (2) What is one area I should approach differently next time?

3. Understand your value.

It is critical to understand how you, in your role, create value for your company. Ask specific questions to learn how leaders in your organization see your contributions adding to the bottom line. These discussions clarify where and how to allocate and focus time and attention and position your ideas and recommendations.

4. Self-advocate.

One of the biggest myths women believe is that their work "speaks for them." It never does, nor will it be the right message. Women need to gain comfort and confidence in discussing their contributions and career goals. Learning to position the message is essential. Share what they are working on and how it impacts the business versus describing tasks completed or busy work occupying time.

5. Lift as you rise.

How do we increase the number of women in organizations? We can actively shine a light on other women by supporting them, getting their voices heard, looking for opportunities to give them visibility to grow and learn, and bringing awareness to crucial decision-makers of their contributions and potential.

DR. SHEILA ROBINSON

FOUNDER, PUBLISHER, AND CEO, DIVERSITY WOMAN MEDIA, *DIVERSITY WOMAN MAGAZINE*

———————

Dr. Sheila Robinson is a celebrated publisher, bestselling author, inspiring speaker, and talent innovation specialist. Her company Diversity Woman Media is recognized nationally as a leading multi-platform enterprise with program offerings that advance all dimensions of diversity and inclusion.

Sheila, an expert in diversity and inclusion, helps leading companies transform their culture to reach gender parity, equity, and belonging by combining her firsthand experience climbing the corporate ladder with the highest academic degrees, best practices from her leading magazines, and a deep passion for evidence-based workplace learnings. She earned a Chief Learning Officer doctor of education from the University of Pennsylvania.

My Five Wisdoms

1. Always see the glass as half full, not half empty.

Throughout my life, I have realized any situation can always be worse. No matter the situation, find a positive in that situation. See the positive side of it, not the negative side.

2. Life is full of lessons and blessings. Always view your outcome as one or the other.

Remove the term "failure" from your mind because we truly learn from our mistakes. In life, we will make mistakes and experience disappointments. Never view them as failures. We learn from every experience in our lives and recognize each one as a lesson that we can learn from and improve on, or if it goes perfectly well, count it as a blessing.

3. Shoot for progress rather than perfection.

We are moving, living, breathing, and growing toward achievable goals if we progress. Perfection is unrealistic and will set you up for disappointment and failure.

4. Strive to not be the smartest one in the room.

When you surround yourself with diverse groups of individuals with different strengths and expertise in areas you don't have, you are positioning yourself to grow, learn, and be challenged.

5. Have empathy.

Empathy is one of the most powerful skills a leader can possess. Leaders are naturally strategic but often neglect to strategize and understand situations when self-absorbed or defensive. Imagine the power of understanding how others are feeling and what others are experiencing and selflessly responding appropriately to a given situation for a positive outcome—the power of empathy.

MONICA SMILEY

**EDITOR AND PUBLISHER,
ENTERPRISING WOMEN MAGAZINE;
PRESIDENT AND FOUNDER,
ENTERPRISING WOMEN FOUNDATION**

Monica Smiley is the Editor and Publisher of *Enterprising Women Magazine*
and the President and Founder of the Enterprising Women Foundation. She
has spent a lifetime devoted to working for the empowerment of women.
As a leader in the women's rights movement in her 20s and 30s and over
the past 22 years as the Founder of a magazine and community, Monica has
empowered, inspired, and educated women entrepreneurs to grow and
scale their companies. She launched the Enterprising Women of the Year
Award more than 20 years ago to spotlight outstanding women entrepreneurs.
This awards program is now considered one of the most prestigious
recognitions for women worldwide. She founded the Enterprising Women
Foundation a decade ago, and its Young Enterprising Women Mentoring
Forum Program has impacted high school girls across the U.S. and Canada.
The recipient of numerous national and global awards, Monica is most
proud of her work to mentor women and girls, including her work with the
PEACE THROUGH BUSINESS program that touches women entrepreneurs
in Afghanistan and Rwanda.

> "Open the door for other women by sharing your wisdom and connections. When women entrepreneurs share their best practices, they empower other women to succeed."

My Five Wisdoms

1. Focus on building relationships.

Relationships are everything in business and life. Nurture friendships and partnerships that help you and others to succeed. When you give back, you receive so much in return, and you feed your soul.

2. Become a part of a community.

The Enterprising Women community has provided me with tremendous fulfillment over the years, wrapping its arms around me when I needed it most. For others, this community has brought meaningful friendships and advice for sustaining and growing a business. There is no need to struggle in business and feel alone.

3. Mentor the next generation.

The work of our nonprofit foundation adds joy and meaning to my life, and everyone who volunteers to be a part of that effort expresses how rewarding it is to them as well. Help a young woman envision what she can be; you will change her life forever.

4. Think global.

The U.S. continues to be a role model for the world regarding women in business. Conferences like the Global Summit of Women and my work with international programs have opened my eyes to the need for us to be advocates for women worldwide. If women ran the world, there would be peace on Earth. Let's make that happen.

5. Have an attitude of gratitude.

Realize that no matter the obstacles in our path, we have the resilience and strength to get through any challenge. If we start each day thankful for what we do have and look for joy in each day—even in the simplest things—we can chase away the negativity that can bring us down.

STEPHANIE SONNABEND

COFOUNDER AND CHAIR, 50/50 WOMEN ON BOARDS

Stephanie Sonnabend is fulfilling her passions of contributing to people's lives and transformational change. She is Cofounder and Chair of 50/50 Women on Boards, the leading education and advocacy campaign driving the movement toward gender balance and diversity on corporate boards.

Stephanie was the President of Sonesta Hotels, a publicly traded, family-controlled business. In her 35-year hospitality career, she built a solid corporate culture applauded by the industry, resulting in the longevity of employees at all levels. Stephanie served on public, private, and nonprofit boards and now teaches women how to position themselves to get on boards of directors.

> "We can do it all, but not all at the same time. We constantly choose between family, career, and self. Embrace your choices without guilt."

My Five Wisdoms

1. Create your personal strategic plan.
Define your passions, set long- and short-term goals, assess your strengths and weaknesses, determine your brand, identify your next steps, and act. In my workshops, I teach women who want to get onto a corporate board that they become an expert in something boards want, and they clearly define their brand. They get board experience through nonprofits, associations, or government commissions. Then, they must let their network know their interest and goals.

2. Make friends, especially women friends.
Nurture your friendships both personally and professionally. Ask how you might help them achieve their goals and demonstrate a genuine interest in their lives. I especially love learning about different cultures and enjoy engaging with people from many parts of the world.

3. Go for it.
Even if you doubt you are qualified for an opportunity, apply anyway. People will see that you are ambitious and interested in career advancement. You will become more confident in your abilities and talents. Love what you do both at work and outside of work.

4. Let it go.
Do not overreact to people making negative comments about you, interrupting, or ignoring you. It reflects poorly on them, not you, and allows you to move on. When people saw that they could not get me rattled, they would often give up.

5. Perform as a leader.
Act as if you are always performing on stage because you are. Look for opportunities to perform as a leader by dressing appropriately, volunteering for high-profile assignments, and demonstrating you are part of the team and the team's leader. Be humble, not arrogant, in your approach. While this was stressful at times, it became easier once I got used to always being in performance mode, and I saw how much I could have a positive impact.

GWEN K. YOUNG

CEO, WOMEN BUSINESS COLLABORATIVE

Gwen K. Young is the CEO of Women Business Collaborative. Gwen is a Visiting Scholar at the Elliot School of International Affairs at George Washington University and former Director of the Global Women's Leadership Initiative at the Wilson Center. An alumna of Smith College, Harvard's Kennedy School of Government, and the University of California, Davis, School of Law, Gwen has pursued a career of international public service focused on humanitarian relief, international development, and human rights. Her career has encompassed a comprehensive array of international organizations, including the Bill & Melinda Gates Foundation, Médecins Sans Frontières, and the International Rescue Committee.

> "I believe that opportunities do not just happen but that you create them. Maya Angelou said, 'As long as you're breathing, it's never too late to do something good.'"

My Five Wisdoms

1. Relationships matter.

Building and maintaining relationships is critical to achieving your professional and personal goals. Relationships offer support, partnerships, and the ability to praise and promote. The key is to build them—meet and connect with people—and maintain them by finding the opportunity to partner and learn.

2. Engage in your community.

We all live and work in a community. Individuals and businesses must be a part of the community in which they live and work. Through this engagement, you will learn about the social norms, systems, and opportunities. Engaging in your community will allow you to develop new skills and have new opportunities.

3. Who you work with matters as much as your job.

Work with people you love, who challenge you and with whom you can collaborate, learn, and grow. These relationships matter as much as what you are working on or doing. Working with people you love helps you build your influence.

4. Be opportunistic.

Be open to new opportunities, jobs, and ideas. Not every career is a straight line. Learning new things involves trying new things.

5. Don't let the past get in the way of your future.

You can learn from past work, mistakes, or successes, but do not let this hold you from moving forward or trying new opportunities. Don't let past mistakes make you doubt your capabilities or possibilities. Use the past as a learning opportunity, and leave it in the past.

JOHANNA (JOSÉ) ZEILSTRA

CEO, GENDER FAIR

Johanna (José) Zeilstra is currently CEO of Gender Fair, a platform that assesses companies on metrics based on the UN Women's Empowerment Principles (www.genderfair.com). Before Gender Fair, Johanna cofounded The Women's Debate to encourage presidential candidates to focus on issues pertaining to women. Johanna also cofounded a corporate social responsibility platform, GiveBack, launched on the *Oprah Winfrey Show* in 2011 and later sold to a large benefit corporation. Johanna runs a Women Entrepreneurs Network and serves on several boards, including the CEO Forum, Princeton Faith & Work Initiative, and Women Business Collaborative.

> "Rather than living by the golden rule of treating others as you want to be treated, live by the platinum rule and treat others as they want to be treated."

My Five Wisdoms

1. Know your power.

With more than half the population, growing access to the world's wealth, and the primary decision-maker of consumer purchases, women have the collective power to close the gap on gender equality. By working for, investing in, and buying from companies that value women, women can communicate that gender equality is no longer a "nice to have" but a business imperative.

2. Focus on your strengths, not your weaknesses.

We are expending unnecessary energy if we focus on fixing our weaknesses rather than improving on our strengths. While we have so many valuable skills and experiences, we spend so much time and resources trying to overcome our limitations that could be directed elsewhere. Focusing on our strengths will bring much more value to achieving our goals.

3. Enlist male allies.

A national survey from Gender Fair indicated that men, across all ages, geographies, and socioeconomic levels, care about gender equality as much as women, if not slightly more. We cannot work toward gender equality without our male allies—especially those in leadership and those with significant influence. They are equally invested in creating a better world for all.

4. Your network is your net worth.

Your network introduces you to opportunities, makes you professionally stronger, and keeps you mentally strong. It becomes your support system during professional challenges. Your network exposes you to new people, ideas, and thoughts, expanding your perception of the world and increasing opportunities to thrive.

5. Make yourself irreplaceable.

Make yourself valuable to your organization, team, and customers. Build skills that no one else can do. You cannot be successful if you are part of a solution that employers or customers will stop investing in if it no longer serves its purpose or if money is tight.

"Believe in yourself, keep the faith, and never lose hope."

—Lilly Ledbetter

CHAPTER 9

PHILANTHROPISTS AND ACTIVISTS MAKING A DIFFERENCE

We all benefit from the purpose and passion of women philanthropists and activists. Two related themes rise to the top in this chapter.

The first is about great female philanthropists who, by investing in others, are helping accelerate the place of women in business and in society. The second is captured through the stories of women activists who spend their days working toward a more equitable and inclusive world.

They truly live their lives preaching that we should believe in ourselves, keep the faith, and never lose hope. They know that giving is the gift that keeps returning to them and in turn leads to growth in others. With their resources and talent, these philanthropic women focus on where they can make change happen. Philanthropists do not need permission to "make a difference."

Activist women express insight and guidance, complementing the philanthropists. These women are devoted to stand with women of all backgrounds and orientations. Yet, as one woman reminds us, "No one sector, entity, or leader can solve complex social challenges, so a good leader must provide a platform for everyone to stand on the leadership stage together." These women turned causes into movements, from political fundraising to parity awareness in justice, sports, or any area of business.

Together, these philanthropists and activists deeply care about the advancement of women. They have strength, fortitude, and persistence to affect change by giving of their time, money, and talent. They also remind us that giving, sharing, and activating others mobilizes people so we all move further, faster, together. Learn from the wisdom of these women who have gone before you, and gain insight to share with those who will come after.

ELIZABETH BIRCH, ESQ.

VICE PRESIDENT, CBRE

Elizabeth Birch is Vice President for the global real estate firm CBRE. She began her career as Director of Litigation and Human Resources Counsel for Apple Computer, Inc. She is also a lifelong member of the LGBTQ community. In the mid-1990s, Elizabeth left her corporate career to head the largest LGBTQ advocacy organization in the United States, the Human Rights Campaign. This instrument became the standard in the U.S. to rate the policies and benefits adopted by most Fortune 1000 companies to allow for the equitable treatment of LGBTQ employees. Elizabeth has been an advisor to many corporations and the Department of Defense and has been a leadership fellow at West Point Academy.

> "Always be willing to venture into foreign territory in all things, for common ground cannot be found clinging to your own island."

My Five Wisdoms

1. Do not be afraid to engage the opposition.

We live in a time of great division. When interaction is reduced to the human level —away from the rhetoric and the airwaves— people can often find common ground.

2. Be yourself.

As a young lawyer, I felt I had to wear the uniform of skirt suits and pantyhose to represent my clients fully. It was only when I shed all that was not me that I became far more powerful in court and public speaking. Authenticity is the watchword.

3. Gratitude is the great driver of goodness.

It is hard to be angry or disappointed while simultaneously being grateful. Each day, find five things you are grateful for and incorporate this ritual into your spiritual practice.

4. Be of service, but remember to reverse engineer systemic bias!

It is not enough to mentor or sponsor those at the margins, including women, particularly women of color. It is necessary to reverse engineer the very systems on which your work institution operates. At times, even small changes to the system can drive profound change. It is essential to deconstruct how opportunities are assigned. Be that advocate for genuine change.

5. Can women have it all?

This was the old debate from the second wave of the modern feminist movement. I had to adjust my career path to rise to the parenting challenge. I would have liked to have been more conscious about this process. It is important to make major life decisions with your eyes wide open. Love with abandon, but prepare for a day when you may be forging life alone or as a single parent. (Yes, this happens in the LGBTQ world as well.) Eventually, your children will grow up, and you can pick up some projects and goals that excited you early in your career.

NOREEN FARRELL

EXECUTIVE DIRECTOR, EQUAL RIGHTS ADVOCATES

Noreen Farrell is a nationally recognized civil rights leader and innovator. She is Executive Director of Equal Rights Advocates, a national nonprofit advancing gender justice through policy reform, litigation, community education, and movement building. Noreen has represented thousands in groundbreaking impact litigation to end discrimination in school and the workplace, including before the U.S. Supreme Court. She is the strategic architect of high-impact campaigns behind dozens of new laws helping millions of women thrive and lead across spheres. Noreen has led the passage of the nation's strongest equal pay laws while also paying it forward as a mother and treasured mentor.

> **"We are the ones we have been waiting for."**
> —American poet, teacher, and activist June Jordan

My Five Wisdoms

1. Demand equality and justice for all, and push yourself to reimagine the American workplace.

Despite gains made for women in the workplace, many experience pay discrimination and harassment. Millions of women were forced from work without adequate paid leave or childcare during the COVID-19 pandemic. Support policies that help women and others remain employed, thriving, and leading even if you have succeeded. Maya Angelou's words resonate: "Because equal rights, fair play, justice, are all like the air: we all have it, or none of us has it."

2. Always trust and lead with your vision of what needs to happen, not what you think you "can get."

The system in which many of us operate posts false limitations: there isn't enough money; that idea is untested; you don't look like a leader; pushing too hard will backfire. Lead beyond the naysayers. By demanding great things, we can achieve them. As Arundhati Roy said, "Another world is not only possible, she is on her way. On a quiet day, I can hear her breathing."

3. Your authenticity is your superpower.

Reject the notion that you must become something or someone else to inspire others. Cherish and share your journey; be self-aware and vulnerable; connect with others with curiosity. The world remembers an original. Do you?

4. Women belong everywhere decisions are being made.

Supreme Court feminist icon Ruth Bader Ginsburg didn't just say these words. She lived them. Find that place women have been excluded, and show up ready to lead. Don't wait for permission. Don't wait your turn. "The most common way people give up their power is by thinking they don't have any."—Alice Walker

5. The test of greatness will not be all you know but all that you share.

Showing gratitude to those who paved your way honors the foundations of our movement. Paying it forward ensures its future. Share what you have learned from your successes and failures; be a mentor and develop new leaders; change the systems that may hold back those who follow you unfairly. These actions are the stuff of sheroes!

CHRISTIE HEFNER

AMERICAN BUSINESSWOMAN AND ACTIVIST

Christie Hefner is an experienced executive and director of both public and private companies. She served for 20 years as Chairman/CEO of Playboy Enterprises, the longest-serving female CEO of a publicly traded company. Christie was widely credited with repositioning the company from its legacy domestic magazine business to a global multimedia and lifestyle company. Over 40 percent of her executives were women.

One of *Fortune*'s Most Powerful Women in the World and a founding member of The Chicago Network and the Committee of 200, Christie serves on the boards of Springboard Enterprises, an accelerator for women tech entrepreneurs, and the Center for American Progress Action, the leading progressive public policy think tank.

> "Don't wait until you're sure you know everything before you try something. 'If you're not in over your head, how will you know how tall you are?'—T. S. Eliot"

My Five Wisdoms

1. Commit to being a lifelong learner.

The days of our lives having three chapters—Learning, Working, and Retirement—are long gone. When considering whether to get involved in helping a company or an organization, one of my criteria is asking: "Will I learn something new?" Intellectual agility is perhaps the most valuable life skill.

2. Learn to be an active listener.

Too often, we think of communication skills as speaking and writing well. These are important, but listening is more than half of it. If you think about what you're going to say when someone else is speaking, you're not listening. Developing the skill to build on others' ideas to knit together the threads in a meeting will make you valued and valuable in many settings, including boardrooms.

3. Find your energy balance.

Years ago, McKinsey interviewed high-performing women to seek to determine commonalities. The dominant one they found was the women's ability to make sufficient time for activities that energized them versus those that sapped their energy. That's different than the old work/life balance, as work can be incredibly energizing, and sometimes family can be draining. Make sure you make time for the things that restore you, whether it's Pilates, listening to music, cooking for friends, or long walks.

4. Develop confidence while remaining humble.

I was demonstrably too confident when, at the age of 29, I told the board of Playboy Enterprises that I was ready to take over that NYSE-traded company, which had just reported a huge loss and had fired its president. Ironically, today, knowing far more, I am also humbler. Finding the right balance is a critical aspect of leadership.

5. Give back not just with time and money but with your experience and expertise.

Get engaged in building networks, community, and our democracy. Whether helping to build the Committee of 200 and The Chicago Network, heading capital campaigns to create a national model for the treatment of HIV/AIDS, a permanent home for the Black Ensemble Theater, or working to elect terrific women candidates, I have been the beneficiary as much as the contributor. Look for ways to have an impact. It's both necessary and enriching.

MEREDITH JACOBS

CEO, JEWISH WOMEN INTERNATIONAL (JWI)

Meredith Jacobs is CEO of Jewish Women International (JWI), a 125-year-old nonprofit dedicated to ending violence against women and girls. Since assuming the role in 2020, Meredith has shepherded the development of the National Center on Domestic Violence in the Jewish Community, the Women's Financial Empowerment Institute, the Jewish Gun Violence Prevention Roundtable, and the international expansion of Young Women's Impact Network. Meredith was named one of the "50 Most Influential Jews of 2020" by the *Jerusalem Post*. Meredith is the former editor-in-chief of *Washington Jewish Week* and author of several bestselling parenting books, including the inspirational book *Just Between Us,* a back-and-forth journal written with her daughter Sofie Jacobs.

> "We do not remember days . . .
> We remember moments."
>
> —Anonymous

My Five Wisdoms

1. Just say "yes." You'll figure out "how."
In my college essay, I wrote about wanting to be Chief Justice of the Supreme Court. Then an advertising executive. I never imagined life doing what I was doing, but I said yes, and life has a way of taking you where you want to go. If I had not said yes, I would not be where I am today as the CEO of a non-profit. Instead of saying, "Why me?" say, "Why not me?"

2. Being nervous or afraid is the same physical feeling you have when excited.
When you are afraid, tell yourself you are excited. Fear can stop you and hold you back. Remember, we don't have time to be afraid.

3. Create opportunities for doors to open.
Opportunity does not knock. You recognize it and make it happen. Don't sit and wait for the world to come to you. Reach out to people and then walk through those doors. Learn to ask for help. Ask for someone's time. Ask for opportunities and position yourself. Find a way to steer a conversation to drop little nuggets about yourself. You are not bragging. Let others get a sense of who you are, so when the time arrives, they just might think of you.

4. Learn from the wisdom of the women who have gone before you, and gain insight to share with those who will come after.
Surround yourself with a community that can walk with you in life and where we can celebrate and support each other. As I have gotten older, female friendships are vitally important. We get so busy with our lives. We need to ensure we have a posse who are there for us as we are mutually there for them.

5. Remember to lift as you rise.
Pave the path for other women and bring them along. Ask yourself, what's the legacy you are building? This is how we build a better world where all women can thrive. When women thrive, we all thrive.

LAURIE KIRKEGAARD

PRINCIPAL, NPL IMPACT AGENCY

Laurie Kirkegaard is co-owner of NPL Impact Agency with her husband, James, pairing philanthropists and leading nonprofit organizations globally, instigating transformational solutions in disease prevention, health, and education. Clients including *National Geographic,* Camp Coca-Cola, the Chan Zuckerberg Initiative, Massachusetts General/Harvard, and the St. John Eye Hospital in Israel credit her for accelerating levels of performance they didn't previously think were achievable by "changing up the game." After decades of speaking and coaching nonprofit boards, CEOs, and donors, Laurie has leveraged over a billion dollars for change and served as a guest teacher at the Goizueta School of Business at Emory.

> "I am relentlessly committed to service above self and never underestimate the power of asking for what you really want. I live by a quote by Wayne Gretzky: 'I miss 100 percent of the shots I never take.'"

My Five Wisdoms

1. Center priorities around the heart.

At age 55, I experienced an unexpected heart attack with no prior symptoms. My life was spared thanks to modern medicine, and I had a defining moment—the wisdom to only focus on people, projects, and issues aligned with my heart. This moment changed how I work and live, keeping passion and purpose in the front row and steering clear of other people's noise.

2. Embrace one day at a time.

I begin each morning with a strong cup of coffee and quiet time to list and reflect on everything I'm grateful for, including the problems I must embrace. That fuels me to stay centered on positively contributing my time and talents daily.

3. You don't get what you don't ask for.

As a company that teaches others how to ask for money, it is one of the greatest fears, along with public speaking. You give a gift when you ask someone to join a worthy cause. You create an opportunity for them to confirm their values, to love and be loved, to leave a legacy, and make a difference in other people's lives. Never be afraid to ask people to contribute their time, talents, and treasures for things that matter.

4. If at first you don't succeed . . . try, try again.

Something I learned firsthand from my parents is that it's critical to keep aim at your target until you achieve it. Innovation comes from constraints, conflict, and new ways to dissect a problem. Like the book *The Little Engine That Could,* if you think you can, (with hard work) you can.

5. Work with smart people who know how to laugh.

I hire people much smarter than me who keep things in perspective and make our team laugh. Laughter makes work and problem-solving more fun and teaches us not to take ourselves so seriously that we forget what it means to add joy to our lives.

THAYER LAVIELLE

**EXECUTIVE VICE PRESIDENT, THE COLLECTIVE,
THE WOMEN'S DIVISION OF WASSERMAN**

Never afraid of a blank page, Thayer Lavielle has built brands and businesses from the ground up. Raised as the only daughter alongside five brothers, her fight for equity started early. It inspired her to shape and launch The Collective—the women-focused practice at global sports and entertainment agency Wasserman. A lifetime of driving impact through community-building, research, insights, and storytelling has shaped her core shared belief that—whether as a person or an organization—you can make more impact together than alone. Passions for travel, play, and family propel her collaborations toward progress.

> "I have asked, 'To what end?' in all-decision making. When explored, this question provides incredible clarity and helps put intention behind your actions."

My Five Wisdoms

1. Don't believe everything you think.

Our minds are powerful tools, and our thoughts are often self-generated storytellers trying to protect us. By seeing these thoughts as optional, you have the power to choose your perspective and opinions differently. So, question long-held beliefs and see what freedom and growth come your way.

2. You can have everything, just not always at the same time.

Being a working mom is a full-time exercise in juggling priorities. The words "relentless, amazing, rewarding" can be applied to work and family, but it's a constant carve-out on one side. It is exhausting to maintain a constant balance, so accept that part of the fun is the up and down.

3. Make the world smaller today.

Make a running list of all the people you want to connect with—friends, family, industry contacts, dream contacts—and set the time to reach out. They'll be happy to hear from you, and you will all feel more connected.

4. Relax.

Apply the rule of five and ask, "Will this matter in five minutes, five days, five months, or five years?" Act accordingly. Too often, women are drawn to the latest fire drill, compelled to solve every issue. By really understanding the lasting importance of something, you assess the level of urgency.

5. Kindness matters.

Perhaps more urgently than ever, we must be intentionally kind to whoever is in front of us, whether we agree with them or not. Spread kindness freely and often; it costs nothing. Besides, a little sugar never hurts a lemon.

LILLY LEDBETTER

ACTIVIST

Lilly Ledbetter, a former supervisor at the Goodyear tire plant in Gadsden, Alabama, discovered that she was being paid 40 percent less than the male managers. She took legal action, and after 10 years of advocating for justice, she became the namesake of President Obama's first piece of legislation, the Lilly Ledbetter Fair Pay Act. An internationally recognized activist, Lilly raises global awareness about equal pay for equal work. She is the coauthor of *Grace and Grit: My Fight for Equal Pay and Fairness at Goodyear and Beyond* and the movie *Lilly,* directed by Rachel Feldman.

> "Every day, I try to make a difference by sharing my story to ensure that what happened to my family and me will not happen to other people and their families."

My Five Wisdoms

1. Women must recognize their retirement begins with their first paycheck.

Pay discrimination is like hypertension—a silent killer. Millions across America, from Main Street to Wall Street, are underpaid simply because they are women. Throughout a 40-year career, women lose approximately $400,000 in their lifetime. Those "pennies" add up, so the minute you start working, you must understand your pay determines your quality of life in retirement.

2. Equal pay for equal work is a fundamental American principle.

We must secure equal pay for our children and grandchildren so that no one will experience the discrimination I did again. Pay discrimination means families cannot afford the necessities in life, whether it's access to proper food, clothing, safe housing, health care, and education. There will be a far richer reward for society if we secure fair pay.

3. Remember your history.

As you experience success and climb the career ladder, remain humble as you interact with your colleagues and employees. Never forget where you came from, personally and professionally.

4. Be proactive.

Equal pay and a fair working environment are not women's but human rights issues. Advocate and speak up for yourself and equal rights in the workplace

5. Believe in yourself, keep the faith, and never lose hope.

Despite the harassment and challenges of working in a tire manufacturing plant, I kept working until I was forced into retirement. But I wouldn't give up then, either. I spent another decade pursuing justice and change. You must have radical resilience to create change. You are not only making a more equitable working environment for yourself but also for future generations.

MICHELLE NUNN

PRESIDENT AND CEO, CARE USA

Michelle Nunn is President and CEO of CARE USA, a global humanitarian organization that works to save lives, defeat poverty, and achieve social justice. Since 2015, Michelle has spearheaded an ambitious strategy to expand impact and revenue, investing in innovative programs, partnerships, and social enterprises.

Before CARE, Michelle built a career of civic and public service as a social entrepreneur, a nonprofit CEO, and a candidate for the U.S. Senate. She cofounded Hands On Atlanta, expanded it into a national network, and led its merger with Points of Light to create the world's largest organization dedicated to volunteer service.

> "Surely, in the light of history, it is more intelligent to hope rather than to fear, to try rather than not to try. For one thing, we know beyond all doubt: Nothing has ever been achieved by the person who says, 'It can't be done.'"
> —Eleanor Roosevelt

My Five Wisdoms

1. Embrace risk.

Fear of failure is almost always worse than actual failure. Every time you fall short, you will learn, grow, and become more resilient. Do something professionally daring on a regular basis, even if you start small. My greatest periods of learning have come from braving defeat—including a run for U.S. Senate that was the best learning experience of my life, despite not winning.

2. Cultivate your relationships with intention.

Ultimately, both our joy and professional progress depend upon our connection to others. Invest in your relationships, and maintain them over the years. Your happiness will directly correspond to the richness of your relationships.

3. Find ways to integrate your family with your work.

While there is no perfect balance between family and work, I found that integrating the two can be enriching and meaningful for everyone. I brought my kids with me to work, service projects, and both my husband and kids traveled with me. This helped them better understand and feel connected to what I was doing when I was away.

4. Stand with women.

Whether mentoring a younger colleague or supporting organizations and policies focused on global gender equality, you will not only find personal gratification advocating for women but you will also lift the tide for everyone. Having worked in the humanitarian industry for years, I can say we have a long way to go in defeating poverty, advancing gender equality, and solving our world's largest crises. The only way to get there will be through women standing with other women.

5. Find ways to use your skills to change the world.

You have a unique set of passions, experiences, and skills that position you to be a catalyst for positive change. When you use those things in service of a cause and purpose that's greater than yourself, you will find true professional success and fulfillment.

DIANE PADDISON

FOUNDER, 4WORD

Diane Paddison is the Founder of 4word, a ministry building a global com-munity of Christian women in the workplace, serving 900,000 in its first 11 years. She is a Harvard MBA and a former international executive of two Fortune 500 companies and one Fortune 1000 company. Diane serves as an Independent Director for one corporation and on the advisory board of a privately held company. She serves on the board of four nonprofit organizations, including The Salvation Army's National Advisory Board. Diane and her husband, Chris, have four adult children and two grandchildren and live in Dallas, Texas, and Portland, Oregon.

> "The only thing we can do is play on the one string we have, and that is our attitude. I am convinced that life is 10 percent what happens to me and 90 percent of how I react to it. And so it is with you . . . we are in charge of our attitudes."
> —Charles Swindoll

My Five Wisdoms

1. Cast a vision others want to follow.
Good leaders won't just dole out "blind" responsibilities to their team. They will share the vision of their ultimate end goal so well that their team will feel compelled to help get them there.

2. Go forward with passion.
Great leaders have a vision. Like Nelson Mandela or Mother Teresa, leaders exude an infectious passion for what they do and how they dream. Your actions will always leave a mark if you lead others with your dreams.

3. Exhibit impeccable character.
Too many leaders are doing incredible things but are doing so at the expense of morals and guidelines. There will be many occasions where a "shortcut" is within reach. Why risk that? What would be more inspiring to you: a leader who had to fight through opposition and roadblocks before succeeding, or a leader who found loopholes and stepped on everyone around them to claw their way to the top? Don't be afraid of struggling. As a leader, struggles are a time for you to grow and be a positive role model.

4. Be accountable.
Accountability is the cornerstone of empowerment and personal growth. Leaders don't just lead their teams. They are a part of their team. Nothing makes team members more invested than seeing that their leader is just like them and is willing to roll their sleeves up and get down to business.

5. Create a legacy today.
All leaders hope deep down that their work and efforts will lead to leaving a legacy. I can't think of a better way to be remembered than by inspiring someone on your team to accomplish something great. Whatever you do as a leader, perform with the hope that your actions will result in someone else's career or life today, tomorrow, and even farther down the road, doing something truly remarkable.

STACEY D. STEWART

CEO, MOTHERS AGAINST DRUNK DRIVING (MADD)

———

Stacey D. Stewart serves as the CEO of Mothers Against Drunk Driving (MADD), the leading organization working to save lives by ending drunk and drugged driving on our nation's roads. Prior to MADD, Stewart served as the fifth president of March of Dimes, the nation's preeminent organization focused on healthy moms and healthy babies. After a 17-year career at both Fannie Mae and the Fannie Mae Foundation, including serving as President and CEO of the Fannie Mae Foundation, Stewart assumed the role of U.S. President of United Way Worldwide. Stewart is married to Jarvis C. Stewart and has two daughters, Madeleine and Savannah.

> "No one sector, entity, or leader can solve complex social challenges, so a good leader must provide a platform for everyone to stand on the leadership stage together."

My Five Wisdoms

1. Women need to be highly valued.
Women need to place an even higher value on their capabilities, their skill sets, and what they bring to any job on the front end. And then, along the way, women must continue to advocate for being paid fairly and acknowledged for their efforts.

2. Women need to get out of the mode of perfectionism—it's a losing proposition.
Women sometimes feel they must complete the job perfectly to prove to everyone beyond the shadow of a doubt that they're capable. The most important thing is to acknowledge that you have value just coming into the workplace daily.

3. Leadership in the nonprofit sector looks like leadership in the for-profit sector.
They both need similar skill sets. We should recruit women from business schools into nonprofits and prepare them for leadership roles.

4. For aspiring women of color, learn from those around you.
When I was the first Black president of the March of Dimes, my advice to up-and-coming leaders of color was to watch and learn from the people around you who are making a positive difference—whether in a professional setting or in their community. As I progressed through my career and took on increasing levels of responsibility, I learned from many others along the way. Watch what others do, then decide what to adopt and adapt for yourself.

5. If you can serve, be a leader.
It's not only a position of privilege. It's a position of responsibility and accountability to others who may be coming behind. We also owe it to the next generation to advocate on their behalf.

SHELLEY ZALIS

FOUNDER AND CEO, THE FEMALE QUOTIENT

Shelley Zalis, Founder and CEO of The Female Quotient, is an internation-ally renowned thought leader, movement maker, and champion of equality. She is a pioneer for online research, becoming the first female chief executive ranked in the research industry's top 25. Today, as CEO of The Female Quotient, Shelley works with Fortune 500 companies and mission-oriented organizations to advance equality in the workplace by creating solutions that close the gender gap across parity, policy, and pipeline. Shelley is a proud mentor to women worldwide and a firm believer in giving back with generosity.

> "Hire for passion and train for skill. You can teach someone how to complete a task, but you can't teach them to care."

My Five Wisdoms

1. No-regret policy.

I never want to look back and say, "shoulda, woulda, coulda," so I always think forward and ask myself the question, "Will I feel bad if I make this decision?" If the answer is yes, I don't do it. No one will ever remember the meeting you missed or the business trip you didn't take, but you, your friends, and your family will never forget the moments that mattered.

2. It's not in a textbook.

I always say, "You have to be the first, the second, and the third." The first is the innovator. There is no textbook to follow, so create the rules. There is no blueprint to follow, so make it up as you go. The second is the copycat, but they don't know what's under the hood, so they are always vanilla. The third is the sweeper. They ride in on the white horse and add the shiny toys, get the money, build on top of the ecosystem, and take the credit. You must be the first, the second, and the third to beat yourself at your own game!

3. Be the chief troublemaker, and break the rules that make no sense.

After all, men made the rules of the workplace for men over 100 years ago. Time to get rid of the junk in the trunk and write the new rules that allow all of us . . . especially caregivers, to thrive in today's workplace with equal opportunity and equal pay. If we create a workplace designed by women, it will work for everyone.

4. Follow your heart, and zig when others zag.

Your head is usually the rationale that may steer you through the status quo, but when you follow your heart, it will take you to that authentic place and allow you to zig when others zag.

5. Bring emotion to the boardroom.

Compassion, empathy, and passion are the most important qualities of leadership today. It's time for invisible skills to be recognized, celebrated, and rewarded.

"Don't wait—start. The universe rewards courage."

—Errin Haines

CHAPTER 10

WOMEN IN THE MEDIA PURSUING PURPOSE WITH PASSION

What can we each learn from the trailblazing, trendsetting, and transformative women in the media industry? These are the women who share their platforms and voices for the betterment of humankind. Their wisdom is insightful and inspiring.

From winning Emmy Awards, to building media networks, to breaking major stories, their vast talents serve as role models for each of us to admire. For most of us, we want to know more about these women who have won those awards, who have been the journalists tracking down the big stories, or who have served as leaders behind the scenes. They teach us to always "show up fully present and ready to play." Or, "If you want something, go after it with everything you've got."

These influential media players provide exceptional role models for the other women following them into a rapidly changing industry. Each woman shows us how to be dedicated, determined, and resilient. They are seen and heard. They remind us that we should know our audience, yours and mine. Wake up each day ready to discover something new, remembering that mistakes are just part of life's learning. Their wisdom is built off their exceptional experiences, which we can learn from.

Women in the media have played an increasingly significant role over past decades. Each has broken the news, led media organizations, and built the next generation of journalists. They envision and produce results at lightning speed, from the airwaves to the sound waves. And each, in their way, cares about how the media portrays women. Their audiences or media outlets may vary, but these women together speak for the well-being, success, and rights of all women. Their wisdom and insights will guide you on how to use your voice and say what you mean and mean what you say.

NADIA BILCHIK

**PRESIDENT, GREATER IMPACT COMMUNICATIONS;
TELEVISION PERSONALITY**

Nadia Bilchik, President of Greater Impact Communications, is an in-ternationally renowned television personality, professional development training expert, author, and keynote speaker. Her insightful and substantive approach to communication skills training comes from her extensive experience in delivering keynote addresses to audiences worldwide, conducting professional development workshops with a roster of multinational corporations, and coaching business professionals. With more than 25 years' worth of television and video experience, Nadia has anchored and hosted feature programs for CNN International, among others, and has interviewed a broad range of high-profile figures, celebrities, and corporate leaders, from Tom Hanks to the late President Nelson Mandela.

> "All women must give themselves permission to become a leader. Nurture your personal presence and ability to override any hesitation or doubt. Make your voice heard, and keep your communication impactful."

My Five Wisdoms

1. Being a masterful communicator takes practice, skill, and will.

It is within all our capabilities, but you need to start with your own self-image. As the French novelist Honoré de Balzac said, "There is no greater impediment to getting on with other people than being ill at ease with yourself." Pay close attention to the conversations you have with yourself, and show yourself the same compassion you would have for a good friend.

2. No one is viewing you with the microscopic lens you turn on yourself.

You don't have to be perfect. Sometimes you just must go for it, experiment, and be OK if it doesn't work out. As Nelson Mandela said, "I never lose; I either win or I learn." When I coach speakers, I remind them that if you do make a mistake, simply say, "Can I rephrase that?" and move on.

3. Be mindful of how you communicate.

Are you projecting warmth and positive energy both in person and virtually? Particularly in the hybrid world we are living in right now, this means being aware of everything from your body language to your facial expressions and your tone of voice. Be mindful and intentional in how you engage others from the moment that camera is on.

4. Read *The Four Agreements* by Don Ruiz Miguel yearly.

It reminds us to not take things personally and to not make assumptions. I like to "assume positive intent," a stance that helps me navigate and defuse difficult conversations by responding in a thoughtful and gracious way.

5. Don't be afraid to take risks.

As science educator Bill Nye says, "Everyone you meet knows something that you don't." Embrace difference and try to see the world from other points of view. You may fail as many times as you succeed, but if you are daring and open to situations that are out of your usual comfort zone, you will surely start to enjoy the journey.

GAIL EVANS

RETIRED EXECUTIVE VICE PRESIDENT, CNN NEWSGROUP; AUTHOR AND SPEAKER

Gail Evans served as one of the highest-ranking female executives at CNN and is the author of *Play Like a Man, Win Like a Woman* and *She Wins, You Win*. An adjunct professor at Georgia Tech's School of Management teaching "Gender, Race and Ethnicity in Global Organizations," she began working at CNN at its inception, in 1980. In 2001, she retired as the Executive Vice President of the CNN Newsgroup.

Gail has served on numerous charitable boards and was appointed by President Clinton to the Commission on White House Fellows. Gail is a member of the Committee of 200 and is on the Council on Foreign Relations. She worked on both the House and Senate staffs and the White House in the Office of the Special Counsel to the President during the Lyndon B. Johnson administration. She was part of the team that created the 1965 Civil Rights Act and the President's Committee on Equal Employment opportunity during her tenure. Gail lives in Atlanta and is the mother of three and the grandmother of seven.

> "As an advocate for women, keeping with the title of my second book—*She Wins, You Win!*"

My Five Wisdoms

1. Show up fully present and ready to play.
Multitasking means you do everything in a mediocre way. When I'm on the playground with a three-year-old, I'm on the playground, and I'm not thinking about a business problem. I'm thinking about playing on the swings, and my mind isn't wandering to the playground when I'm in the office. Most people are only partially there, whether it's home or the office.

2. Understand a breakdown, and grow from it.
Life, especially business, is a series of breakdowns. Don't waste your time blaming others. Concentrate on what happened, not why. "Why" is usually about judgment. "What" is about information. Ask yourself what you did to contribute to the problem, and learn from that lesson. You played a role in it, no matter how small. Also, remember to cut your losses fast. Request to see what's possible, and don't assume anything. Don't keep holding on and trying to fix something unfixable.

3. Remember, "no" is just a piece of business information.
Don't let it stop you or your ideas. "No" is the first word in the strategy of getting to "yes." I love being strategic. It's the key to business and personal success too.

4. Be strategic in your career.
If asked, take positions you aren't always qualified for, as that is how leaders grow.

5. Learn to embrace the word "power," and use it as a force for good.
You can make a living and make a difference at the same time.

CHERYL GOULD

AWARD-WINNING BROADCAST JOURNALIST

Cheryl Gould, Senior Vice President, *NBC News* **(retired), is an award-**winning American journalist whose career spanned almost four decades at the network. As the first female Executive Producer of a network nightly newscast, she is known as a pioneer, role model, and mentor for women in the industry making newsrooms more diverse. Cheryl is a Board Member of the Committee to Protect Journalists and has been the Jury Chair of the Columbia University Journalism School's duPont Awards. She is a graduate of Princeton University, received a diploma from the Sorbonne, and is a member of the Council on Foreign Relations.

> "We excel when we help others grow. Hire people you believe have the potential to do the job as well as you can one day."

My Five Wisdoms

1. Keep in mind that your coworkers and your direct reports are each the sum of many parts.

People have good days and bad, successes and failures, problems at home, family joys, and many concerns unrelated to work. They don't come to work in a vacuum. It is important to see them as real people. The more you can recognize that they exist beyond the office, the more empathy you show—without being overly personal—the more productive and loyal they will be.

2. Be open to all ideas, no matter how offbeat they may strike you.

It's important that your team feel they can brainstorm out loud without fear of being ridiculed or shot down. Don't reject the ideas out of hand. Urge the presenter to flesh out their ideas in front of the group.

3. Act decisively, and give responses in a timely manner.

Respond to emails and phone messages and encourage others to do the same. Don't assume that because you are cc'd, you don't need to acknowledge the note.

4. Give regular feedback—both positive and negative.

If negative, make sure it's done respectfully and with advice for improvement. Invite them to give suggestions for how you and the company could do things better, and if the ideas are worth implementing, do so!

5. Be kind, be flexible, have an open door, be fair, be trustworthy.

If you oversee a large group, walk the halls and get to know as many of your staff as possible. The buck really does stop with you, so don't blame others if things go awry. And do not take credit for other people's ideas and work. It is better to be recognized by your bosses or board for creating and maintaining a hospitable workplace in which people can do their best work and contribute to the overall success of the company than it is to take all the credit for the successful ideas and implementation.

ERRIN HAINES

FOUNDING MOTHER AND EDITOR-AT-LARGE,
THE 19TH; MSNBC CONTRIBUTOR

Errin Haines is a Founding Mother and Editor-at-Large at *The 19th,* a nonprofit, independent newsroom focused on the intersection of gender, politics, and policy. She is also an MSNBC contributor. Prior to joining *The 19th,* Errin was the national writer on race and ethnicity for the Associated Press and has previously worked at the *Washington Post,* the *Los Angeles Times,* and the *Orlando Sentinel.* Errin serves on the board of the Lenfest Institute for Journalism and has taught classes on race, gender, and politics at Georgetown University and Princeton University.

> "Am I doing work that meets the moment, in the place where it will have the most impact?"

My Five Wisdoms

1. Don't wait—start. The universe rewards courage.

2. At the beginning of your career, your power is in your ability to say yes. Later in your career, your power is in your ability to say no.

3. Ask yourself, "Am I stuck, or do I just need a nap?"

4. Make up your mind, then let it go.

5. Grace is something you can also give yourself.

JOANNE LaMARCA MATHISEN

BUSINESS LEADERSHIP COACH; FORMER EXECUTIVE PRODUCER, *NBC NEWS/TODAY*

Joanne LaMarca Mathisen is an Emmy Award-winning morning show producer. She began her career in NBC's esteemed Page Program, giving studio tours and seating audiences. After just a few months, Jo moved to NBC's *Today,* where, throughout her career, she went from Production Assistant to Executive Producer, with stops at CBS, the *Wall Street Journal,* and CNBC. In September 2022, Jo signed off as *Hoda & Jenna*'s Executive Producer to start something new. Now she's consulting and working with managers to help them realize their fullest potential.

> "If you want something, go after it with everything you've got. If it doesn't pan out, there's something better waiting to happen. Not everybody wins a trophy at the same time."

My Five Wisdoms

1. Always be willing to do the work.
There's always someone more competent or with better connections, but not everyone is willing to do the work. Be willing, be open, and don't be afraid to show them what you're made of. Know your place, but don't live by the boundaries.

2. We all have a story.
Employees aren't just employees. Coworkers aren't just coworkers. Take time to know the people you work with and those who work for you, especially those who work for you. Listen to their stories. Understand who they are and where they've come from. When you listen, you'll understand them better and learn something about yourself.

3. Jump before you're pushed.
I learned this years ago from someone I highly respect. It's like leaving the party when you're having fun. If you feel things are headed south in your environment or with your position and you have an opportunity to explore something new, explore. Those moments are often the universe leading you to the next step in your career.

4. Stick it out. Not every job is a dream job.
But the harder they are, the more we learn and the more we prove to ourselves what we're capable of. I'm not saying to stay if the working situation is intolerable, but often people run when they're feeling out of their comfort zone. Don't run. Learn. Then run!

5. Say "please" and "thank you."
You've heard there's power in numbers. As you journey through your career, remember the people you enjoyed working with and those you learned from. Make sure to tell them how you feel. Write them a note or give them a call. It will mean so much to them and make you feel good to share your feelings. It's also good to have as many people in your corner as possible; you never know where your next lead will come from.

LISA MATTHEWS

ASSOCIATED PRESS, U.S. NEWS PLANNING EDITOR

Lisa Matthews is a 20-plus-year Associated Press veteran. In 2021, Lisa became the 114th President of the National Press Club, leading the club's first-ever all-women leadership team, reaching historically Black colleges and universities, and offering journalism/communications graduates free one-year memberships. Previously, Lisa worked in public relations as Vice President at Hager Sharp. Matthews earned two Edward R. Murrow Awards—in 2002 for outstanding coverage of September 11, 2001, and in 2010 for Video Continuing Coverage of the Economy. Matthews was the first working journalist inducted into the National Capital Public Relations Society of America (PRSA) Hall of Fame. She received her B.A. in communications from James Madison University.

> "Speak up and be an advocate for others. For years, I have lived with MS (multiple sclerosis) and used my voice to shine a light on a community that often feels marginalized and unseen."

My Five Wisdoms

1. Know your audience.

Understanding the people in the room is key to connecting and ultimately succeeding. The same applies to the media, work, and in life. Someone is always watching, listening, or taking notes. While we earn respect and people's trust over time, never do so at the cost of your dignity, integrity, and values.

2. Wake up with a smile.

A smile is a natural boost; to me, it's better than a cup of coffee. Even if the sun is not shining, it must shine inside us to keep our day going. I've been accused of being a crazy morning person because I'm happy and love what I do. I start my day on a positive note, and the rest follows.

3. Look before you leap.

Instead of reacting, I have learned to pause, think, and, yes, even write down the positives and negatives. Do it before you jump, and read your answers out loud. Ask yourself, why are you making this choice? What are the benefits? Can you turn that situation into a win?

4. Have a go-to gal.

When I face any obstacle, I ask myself, what would my mom do? I am fortunate to be able to call her. She is my reality check, and I run by her first in everything I do. My mom has given me the strength and encouragement to say what I think and is my sounding board. Everyone needs a friend, a mentor, or someone who shares honest feedback and a keep-it-real perspective.

5. Celebrate other people's accomplishments.

I have a cowbell at my desk, and I ring that bell proudly and loudly every time a colleague's story is picked up. Everyone knows when Lisa's cow bell rings, someone on our team has succeeded. I want everyone to share that pride every single day.

PAT MITCHELL

COFOUNDER, CONNECTED WOMEN LEADERS FORUMS; COFOUNDER, HOST, AND CURATOR OF TEDWOMEN

Throughout her career as a journalist, Emmy-winning producer, and pioneering executive, Pat Mitchell broke new ground for women, elevating representation, stories, and ideas. She continues today as the Cofounder of Connected Women Leaders, a cohort of global leaders committed to collective problem-solving. In her memoir, *Becoming a Dangerous Woman: Embracing Risk to Change the World,* Pat defines "dangerous" as a commitment to speak up for the unrepresented, to speak out against abuse and injustice, and to show up for others. Pat's life and work model is how to share power and the difference each of us can make in shaping an equitable, sustainable world.

> "Willingness to take risks and fail is necessary to finding success. My grandmother said, 'Falling on your face is at least a forward movement!'"

My Five Wisdoms

1. Take risks.

Taking risks is not as easy as it sometimes sounds and is more important than it may seem. But it's essential to be willing to take risks to grow, learn from experience, and move forward.

2. Learn by doing.

Women often think we must know everything, have done everything before, and tick all the boxes on an application. Not true. Just say YES to the challenges and learn by doing.

3. Select the best mentor, and be a responsible mentee.

Mentors or sponsors should be people you admire and want to emulate. Be respectful of their time commitment by showing up prepared with specific asks and then pass it on by becoming a mentor to someone else.

4. Make your leadership hires and fires early in your tenure in a position.

Every leader needs the right team for support, and if you wait, hoping the team will come together, it wastes time.

5. Women have the opportunity as leaders to change the nature of power rather than power changing the nature of women.

We have different attributes, life stories, and ways of leading and working, and bringing our whole selves to our work produces the best results. One of the best ways to change the nature of power is to share it and use it to empower and elevate others.

CHRISTINE PULLARA

TALK SHOW HOST AND MEDIA PERSONALITY

———

Christine Pullara has worn many hats with over 30 years in television. From award-winning news anchor to a freelance journalist, commercial/voice-over actor, and model, Christine has covered news, sports, fashion, education, and entertainment. In 1999, Christine hosted HGTV's *Treasure Makers*. She then spent several years as a television host and producer in Los Angeles, working on shows for E! Entertainment, FOX, and the Fine Living Network. In 2005, she moved to Atlanta to host *Bushwhacked* on Turner South, which earned two Southeast Emmy Awards. Christine has hosted *Atlanta & Company* weekdays for over a decade on 11-Alive, Atlanta's NBC affiliate.

> "Be a FORCE for change, for good, and others. Stay passionate about telling stories in a way that informs, educates, and entertains."

My Five Wisdoms

1. Take a sincere interest in others.
Don't be disingenuous! At my first television station, WFLA TV, in Tampa, they had us read *How to Win Friends and Influence People* by Dale Carnegie. His principles are still applicable almost a century later. I genuinely love learning about people and their experiences and realities. That sincere curiosity has sustained me throughout my career.

2. Don't worry, but do prepare.
Whether freelancing and worrying about my next job or prepping for a big celebrity interview, I had to learn how to battle the beasts of fear, doubt, and worry. Be prepared. The preparation leads to confidence, which leads to success!

3. Never burn a bridge.
If a show was canceled or I was the one ready to move on, I tried to convey my sincere appreciation for the opportunity and the valuable experience I learned. Every experience has been unique. Some have been grand on a national scale, some smaller that never made it past the edit room. All of them have taught me unforgettable life lessons. If you're meant to work with a team or show again,

you'll be so happy you left professionally, and hopefully, memories of your work ethic will linger.

4. Show gratitude. Say "thank you."
"Thank you" are such small words with monumental significance. Every day, I thank my guests, crew, team, and even bosses because I know how great it feels to be acknowledged for a job well done. Go one step further and drop them a good old-fashioned note. I promise they won't forget it!

5. Evolve.
In college, I was splicing and taping film images together. How far we've come. Now we can record and edit incredible images right on our phones. It's sometimes tricky keeping up with the changing times, but it's also an exciting challenge. I love helping and mentoring young women, but they keep me on my toes and help me adapt to new technologies and trends.

ELIZABETH RALPH

EDITOR, *POLITICO MAGAZINE*

Elizabeth Ralph is the editor of *POLITICO Magazine*, an award-winning magazine covering the people, places, and ideas shaping American politics. Elizabeth helped found the magazine as an assistant editor in 2013 and quickly moved up the ranks to become editor in 2022. She is also the editor of "Women Rule," *POLITICO*'s journalism and events series covering women, politics, and power, and previously wrote the *Women Rule* newsletter. Elizabeth has been an International Strategy Forum fellow, is deeply curious, and loves acting, travel, and skiing. She once retraced Hannibal's 218 BC campaign over the Alps.

> "Be yourself. I found my greatest career success when I started leaning into what makes me different from other people rather than what makes me the same."

My Five Wisdoms

1. Life is not a race.

The sooner you stop comparing yourself to others, the trajectories of their lives, and the speed of their accomplishments, the better. Life is about finding a path and career arc that works for you; the burdens of status anxiety and meaningless gold-star chasing will only distract you. Don't be afraid to explore new opportunities, change paths, and take breaks!

2. Build a group of advisors, and appreciate them.

One of the most rewarding parts of my career has been finding a group of advisors—mentors, friends, guides—whose opinions I rely on and trust and who genuinely want the best for me (as I do for them). Don't force these relationships—build them on genuine camaraderie—and don't hesitate to tell your advisors how much you appreciate their support.

3. Stay curious.

Nurture an intense curiosity about yourself, the people around you, and the world more broadly. It will make work and life more interesting, open doors, and send opportunities your way.

4. Write a vision statement.

I used to think I had to "figure out what I wanted to do with my life." Now that I know I cannot plan life out in one session, I instead write a vision statement—just one sentence spelling out not the career I want to have but the kind of person I want to be and the kind of life I want to live. I go after opportunities that help me achieve my vision and say no to the ones that don't. And when I decide I need a new one, I can rewrite it!

5. You have more power than you think.

A few years ago, I decided something I wanted to do was impossible. "They'll never let me do that," I told my mentor. "Elizabeth, there is no 'they,'" he responded. It was a good lesson: Don't give up your power by assuming someone will stop you before you even try. You'll likely find that no one will stop you.

"Every great dream begins with a dreamer. Always remember, you have within you the strength, the patience, and the passion to reach for the stars, to change the world."

—Harriet Tubman

ACKNOWLEDGMENTS

As with everything in life that is important, nothing is done without a world of individuals helping and women supporting women. This book reflects the generous spirits and unlimited support that we have received.

It is with deep appreciation that we thank those who helped us blaze the trail to bring *Women Mean Business* to life. As we honor the extraordinary women featured in this book, we are proud to share how they paved the way for other women and demonstrated that women mean business and business needs women.

We feel especially grateful to have united with each other as a dedicated team. This book was accomplished through this collaborative effort, which we, as women in business, understand and truly value. We wish to thank our dedicated husbands, Joe Oppenheimer (Edie), Ed Gerson (Robyn), and Andy Simon (Andi), and our beloved family and friends, who cheered us on during the months spent writing this book.

To Meredith Bernstein, whose seasoned literary agenting acumen supported us in making this book a reality. Meredith recognized the importance of women helping other women thrive and has demonstrated decades of making a difference with her laser-focused ideas, persistence, and support. And to Katharine Sands, for her guidance and wisdom.

To our talented editor, Jean Lucas, our publishing champion, who has gone to great lengths to create and design a book that would impact and change lives to help women succeed in business and in life. It has been our good fortune to work on this book with Jean and the entire publishing team at Andrews McMeel with the goal to brighten and enlighten the world of women at work.

Our endless thanks to the hundreds of supporters of this mission who have generously helped us reach our goals and uplift businesswomen every day. To the visionary women profiled, thank you for accepting the nomination to be included. To countless luminaries, advocates, assistants, and contacts who offered their generous assistance and support along the way, we are deeply grateful for the help you have given us to bring this book to life. We also thank these women leading companies and organizations as they advance gender leadership and diversity. We appreciate and honor you in our lives.

We believe that gratitude is not just an attitude; it's a way of life. We express our joy for this committed community. As Helen Keller said, "Alone we can do so little; together we can do so much." There is pride in sharing a passion for elevating one another. We acknowledge each of you as major advocates.

Photo Credits

Page 4: Omega World Travel, Inc.

Page 6: Heather Moore

Page 8: First Element Conference; First Element

Page 10: Violetta Markelou

Page 12: AP Images for Siemens; Siemens USA

Page 16: The Branded Boss Lady

Page 18: Jack Soltysik

Page 19: EDENS

Page 24: Courtesy Diversified Search Group

Page 36: Tony Valadez Photography

Page 48: Independence Health Group

Page 54: Kara Macko Photography

Page 56: bottom photo, Manuela Rana

Page 62: Linkage, Inc.

Page 66: Jason McCoy Photography

Page 68: IBM

Page 78: SCORE Foundation

Page 80: Gwen Flowers

Page 84: Alvin Gee Photography

Page 90: Rebecca Mitchell Photography

Page 92: Michael Preston Design

Page 94: Anthony Mongiello

Page 98: Dokk Savage Photography

Page 102: Joseph V. Labolito

Page 104: Mary Jane Starke

Page 108: Thurner Photography

Page 110: Augusta Blair Portraits

Page 112: Stephanie Marie Photography

Page 114: Bailey Tillman, KNOCK Inc.

Page 116: Ann-Margaret Johnson Photography

Page 118: Cameron Lee

Page 122: Courtesy Jazzercise, Inc.

Page 126: George Lange

Page 130: Marla Aufmuth, Getty Images

Page 142: Ben Archer

Page 144: Getty Images

Page 148: Eric Millette

Page 150: Dorly Roy, Goldenlight Creative

Page 156: Courtesy The Tyler Twins

Page 158: Douglas Gorenstein

Page 166: Diane Bondareff Photography; bottom photo, Lasting Impressions Photography

Page 168: Frank Veronsky

Page 170: Fábio Câmara Studios

Page 182: Marissa Rauch Photography

Page 184: Charles Revell

Page 188: Michael Bennett Kress Photography; bottom photo, Jules Jacobs

Page 190: Eric Bern, Headshot Studio Atlanta

Page 194: Vickie Saxon

Page 196: CARE

Page 200: March of Dimes

Page 210: NBC News official photo

Page 212: Vanessa Cerday Photography

Page 216: Sam Hurd Photography

Page 220: Sara Hanna Photography

Page 230: Bottom photo, Keiko Guest Photography

Page 231: Howard Copeland Photography

Index of Contributors

ABOUT THE AUTHORS

Edie Fraser is a trailblazing change leader, entrepreneur, and philanthropist, respected for her passionate and purposeful advocacy for gender and diversity. She is a Founder and first CEO and current Chairman of Women Business Collaborative (www.wbcollaborative.org), the women business movement, a nonprofit to accelerate equal position, pay, and power for all businesswomen. She was Founder of STEMconnector and its Million Women Mentors (MWM) initiative, the Public Affairs Group, and Diversity Best Practices and is proud of her 12 years at Diversified Search Group. With 71 major awards for leadership, gender, and diversity advocacy, she was saluted by the CEO Forum Group with its 2022 Gender Leadership award. Inducted into the Enterprising Women Hall of Fame, she received its Legacy award, and she is one of the chairs of the Young Enterprising Women Foundation's STEM program. She received the Mosaic Award from Diversity Woman. Edie served on the board of SCORE and received its leadership award, today supporting SCORE Foundation's gender leadership for women. She was the first woman Chair of the World Affairs Council of Washington, DC, and is a founding and current Board Member of C200. Edie coauthored *Do Your Giving While You Are Living* with Robyn Freedman Spizman. Edie's other books include *Women's Entrepreneurship in America*. In 2015, she released *Advancing a Jobs-Driven Economy* with STEMconnector®, *WOW Facts*, and *Women's Quick Facts*. She produced many books and reports related to diversity, including *The Chief Diversity Officer* and *The Diversity Primer*.

Robyn Freedman Spizman is an award-winning *New York Times* bestselling author and well-known and accomplished media personality. Authoring over 75 inspirational, career, and nonfiction books, she appeared as a popular guest for over three decades on Atlanta's NBC affiliate WXIA-TV, repeatedly on NBC's *Today* show, and has been featured extensively in the media. A seasoned communications expert with four decades of publishing success, she earned her way into the highly competitive field of book writing. Her books include *Loving Out Loud: The Power of a Kind Word, When Words Matter Most, Do Your Giving While You Are Living* (with Edie Fraser), and *Don't Give Up . . . Don't Ever Give Up* with her son Justin Spizman. Robyn also cowrote a series of career books for women, including *Take This Book to Work* and *Will Work from Home* with Tory Johnson, plus *A Hero in Every Heart* with literary icon H. Jackson Brown Jr. and parenting books with Drs. Stephen and Marianne Garber. Robyn's timely consumer suggestions and books have been featured by major media outlets, including CNN and MSNBC; numerous ABC, NBC, CBS, and Fox affiliate stations; as well as the *New York Times, USA Today, USA Weekend, Woman's Day, Ladies' Home Journal, Family Circle,* and *Parade* magazine. A communications professional and popular keynote speaker, she has entertained audiences across the country. The loves of Robyn's life are her husband, children, grandchildren, family, and friends, whom she credits as her everything. www.robynspizman.com.

Andi Simon, PhD, is an international leader in the growing field of corporate anthropology and is the CEO of Simon Associates Management Consultants. Andi is an award-winning author of two bestselling books. *On the Brink: A Fresh Lens to Take Your Business to New Heights* was the Axiom Bronze Best Business Book of 2017 in the Operations Management/Lean/Continuous Improvement category, and *Rethink: Smashing the Myths of Women in Business* was a 2022 Bronze Best Business Book for the Women in Business category. Andi uses anthropology's theory, methods, and tools to enable organizations to see their organizational cultures through a fresh lens. Her talks titled "Change Matters" and "Blue Ocean Strategy" have been featured in hundreds of engagements globally. Andi's thought leadership is widely covered in *Inc.com, Bloomberg Businessweek, Good Morning America,* and *Modern Healthcare,* and she has been a blogger for *Forbes, HuffPost* and *Fierce Healthcare.* Her podcast, *On the Brink with Andi Simon,* ranks among the top 5 percent of global podcasts (www.andisimon.com/podcast). A woman deeply committed to the Women Business Collaborative, Andi has built an annual conference on rethinking women in business. She also specializes in coaching women to excel as leaders. Andi is a devoted wife, proud mother and grandmother, and an avid horsewoman, golfer, and explorer. www.simonassociates.net.

At time of printing, every effort has been made to provide current titles of all contributors.

Andrews McMeel Publishing
a division of Andrews McMeel Universal
1130 Walnut Street, Kansas City, Missouri 64106
www.andrewsmcmeel.com

23 24 25 26 27 SDB 10 9 8 7 6 5 4 3 2 1

ISBN: 978-1-5248-8050-7

Library of Congress Control Number: 2023933058

Editor: Jean Z. Lucas
Art Director: Tiffany Meairs
Production Editor: Elizabeth A. Garcia
Production Manager: Jeff Preuss